TAKE CARE
OF YOUR HORSE

TAKE CARE
OF YOUR HORSE

*A Guide to the Essentials
for Everyone Who Rides, Owns,
or Hopes to Own a Horse*

MARCIA S. COPPER

Charles Scribner's Sons NEW YORK

Photographs by Drew Davenport
Drawings by Francis W. Davis

Library of Congress Cataloging in Publication Data

Copper, Marcia S
    Take care of your horse.
    1. Horses. I. Title.
SF285.3.C66   636.1'08'   74–540
ISBN 0-684-15375-0

1 3 5 7 9 11 13 15 17 19 H/P 20 18 16 14 12 10 8 6 4 2

Contents

Preface

Horses are becoming more and more popular in this country. Some people are getting on them for the first time; others are returning to the sport they once loved and are enthusiastically introducing it to their children. For this reason, I have tried to write a book reaffirming many important fundamentals which are too often forgotten, even by experienced horsemen. *But they must not be forgotten if the horse is to be healthy and happy.*

I do not intend this book to be an absolute manual. It is a guide. Common sense and knowledge of one's own horse must always play a part in any decisions. I strongly suggest throughout the book that expert help be sought when in doubt. A simple phone call to a vet or to a good professional horseman can often save the amateur long hours of work or the possibility of injury.

Although most people wish to buy a horse they can keep and enjoy for years, the turnover in horses is amazing—mostly, I believe, because the reason for purchasing the horse is not clear in the buyer's own mind. I have attempted to help solve this problem.

Above all, I have tried to help the reader understand his horse—how he thinks and feels and why he does what he does, both in the barn and under saddle—and to point out the potential difficulties and dangers that most commonly occur.

I feel that most books of this type already published are too long. They are filled with various bits and pieces, all informative, but not necessary to the actual care and consideration of the horse. As a result the reader tends to skim over pages and thus can miss something important. One must always start at the beginning and work his way up. The beginning but never to be forgotten facts are the essence of this book.

Horses have been a special part of my life for almost as long as I can remember. Today my husband, three children, and I live in a crooked 150-year-old farmhouse surrounded by two dogs, one cat, two goldfish and three very individual horses: Pushover, our brainy grey mixed breed; Lot's Moore (Sam, to his friends), our playful registered Quarter Horse; and Son of Junior, our once sickly Thoroughbred from off the track. It has been my good fortune to have met, made friends with, and learned from some of the most highly respected and knowledgeable professional and amateur horsemen and horsewomen in the country. And I am still learning.

I hope that all would-be riders and owners will read and enjoy this book. I hope that all experienced horsemen will take pleasure in reviewing old principles and in sharing my misadventures with the horse. I'll wager they can match me story for story.

TAKE CARE
OF YOUR HORSE

1

Responsibility
of the Horse-Owner

Life for the horse-owner has changed in many ways since World War II. In the past most owners had grooms to care for their horses. Now the person who grew up waiting at the stable door for his horse to be brought to him finds he must learn how to saddle and bridle his own. Many of today's owners are building small stables and are caring for their animals themselves. Therefore they must learn how to feed, stable, and clean them, none of which is easy. Proper care entails time, patience, and lots of work. Fortunately, half the pleasure and benefit of owning a horse comes from keeping him in your own backyard. The owner has a far better opportunity to know and understand his horse, as does his horse to know and respond to him.

Although people who work with and ride on horses should do at least some research, many people wish neither to take the time, nor do they have the sincere interest, to delve deeply into the study of horses. The horse is thought of mostly as a pleasant form of conveyance and a means to enjoying good sport with one's friends. Which he is.

But there are some basic principles that a person must learn if he wishes to be successful in keeping a horse. Fundamentally it is of no importance whether a horse is a high-class purebred or a simple nobody. He still reacts with the same instincts, he responds to the same body comforts.

Morally, every horse-owner has an obligation toward his horse. When he eats, where he eats, where he lives, where he goes; every decision regarding the welfare of the horse depends upon his owner. The horse living in his natural state knew how to defend and fend for himself. Enclosed in a barn and domesticated for human use, the horse is forced to rely upon his owner for decent care. Horse-owners must recognize and accept this fact. It makes no difference whether the horse lives at home or is boarded in a stable somewhere nearby. It is the owner's duty either to carry out himself the responsibilities he has accepted when purchasing a horse or, at the least, to be able to identify them so as to be sure that his horse is cared for properly by others.

Very briefly let me state a few of the most important principles involved. In further chapters each is enlarged upon and explained.

—A horse should be fed grain at least twice a day. He should be supplied with ample forage (i.e., good grass and other nutritious foliage) or he should be supplied with hay. He should have water and salt available at all times.

—A horse should be protected from the elements if they become too severe.

—A horse is happier and far more secure if he remains on a regular feeding and exercise schedule day after day after day. To put it bluntly, that means he cannot be left to his own devices the weekend you have decided to take a ski trip or to go visit Aunt Susie. The owner with a conscience doesn't neglect even a morning or evening feeding just because he happens to be tired.

—A horse's hooves are very much like our finger- and toenails. They grow, and as a result, need filing and care. About every five to eight weeks a farrier (more commonly called a blacksmith) should be called to care for the horse's feet and shoes or eventually the horse may become lame.

—Horses, like any other animal, have worms. These parasites must be kept under control or they will kill. There are all kinds of worm medicines on the market, but the most effective and often-times cheapest deterrent is to have a veterinarian come at least twice a year to worm the horse thoroughly.

—Yearly flu and tetanus shots are essential.

The person who is not willing to accept these responsibilities should not own a horse. If he wants someone else to see to his horse's daily care, he should place the horse in the most reliable stable he can find and depend upon them to care for him.

Either way horses are expensive and they WILL tie you down.

A horse needs and wants a friend.

2

About the Horse

You will get along better with your horse and he will be happier if you are aware of certain characteristics of the horse in general.

First of all, most horses have excellent memories. They also are extremely sensitive to the people around them and usually, thank heavens, wish to please. These characteristics help to a great extent in training and managing them.

Horses have distinct personalities. And their abilities vary. Some horses are more athletic, some more high-spirited, some more timid, and some "just plain simpleminded." An astute horseman learns to recognize his own horse's particular talents and limitations and uses them to his advantage.

Horses are gregarious. In their natural state they ran free, but always in herds. If they had their choice, of course, they still would today. They have always gained confidence from one another (although it is also true that if one horse becomes frightened, others may react to his fear). One lone horse may be very unhappy when asked to leave a group of horses until he has been well trained. If given the opportunity, the horse who lives by himself will adopt a dog or a goat or some other animal as a companion. He needs and wants a friend to give him confidence and to help break the monotony of a dull day.

Several horses together in a field are interesting to watch, because they have their own variety of pecking order. There is always one who is the leader. It is not only stallions who fight for the right to lead. A new horse in a pasture endures a terrible existence until the horses have decided among themselves who will lead and who will follow. The fights can be bloody, since horses use their teeth as well as their heels. Even after all the members of the group have been assimilated, there are friends and there are foes within the group.

An object seen by a horse's eyes is many times enlarged and distorted compared to the same one seen by ours. Because a horse's eyes are placed more to the side than to the front, he has peripheral vision and the ability to see two separate things coming toward him at the same time—one on either side of his body. Until he is able to focus both eyes on one object, he may respond by fussing and fidgeting. To him, that small rock along the wayside appears to be a huge boulder. A fluttering piece of paper becomes a real danger. A still object is sometimes more frightening to him than a moving object because it can be more difficult to identify. However, when given reassurance and time to become familiar with the object, the horse eventually relaxes.

Naturally the horse's mental processes do not work as quickly or as efficiently as ours. This past year my quarter horse, Sam, was introduced to the hunt field. He was terribly nervous but doing his best to obey. In time we met a particularly muddy jump. He had already begun his takeoff when his hind feet slipped out from underneath him. Somehow he managed to make the jump, but received a terrible rap on both hind legs for his trouble. Poor guy! It was not within his immediate realm of understanding to realize that he had only slipped, that the situation would probably not happen again. As a result, the next time Sam jumped "high enough to reach the moon," even though the ground was perfectly dry and the jump was no higher than any of the previous ones he had taken.

One horse in a group is *always* the leader.

We must be ready for and try to understand the limitations of a horse's reasoning powers.

A horse is blessed with a marvelous sense of hearing and his sense of smell is acute. He relies upon these senses for his safety almost as much as on his sight. He will smell a deer or pheasant long before you can see it. Because his hearing is so sensitive, loud or unfamiliar noises often spook him. His natural instinct when he is frightened is to jump and run; and this he will do.

A horse has a will and desires of his own much as a small child does. It is certainly obvious, for example, that being in a nice green pasture or a comfortable stall is more inviting to a horse than having someone saddle and bridle him to travel through heaven knows what. The person who works with horses must be patient and understanding, but at the same time he must insist upon obedience both in the barn and under saddle. Clever horses will try to get their own way. If they are successful the first time, they will try again and again. Spoiled, disobedient, unmannerly horses are not uncommon. Unfortunately, spoiled horses can be dangerous. They go where they want to go, do what they want to do, regardless of their owner's wishes or sometimes even their own safety.

For the most part horses are animals of steady habits. A schedule is part of their security. Once again, watch the pasture. You will discover that they prefer to sleep, eat, exercise and play at nearly the same time every day. A horse-owner will find his animals much easier to care for if he respects their desire for routine. If he feeds the same time every day, they'll be waiting for him. If he gives them the same stall each day, they'll go into it willingly. If he respects their time for sleeping and eating, they'll give him a far more responsive ride. Of course, a horse's schedule can be arranged to fit his owner's. He really doesn't care what time he eats, sleeps, and works as long as there is a routine which he can rely upon.

If given the opportunity and the room horses like to play. Most are inquisitive and curious. Some are just plain nosy. Especially if something new has been added to their own territory. Our three can be ridiculous.

When my husband tries to plow he is accompanied by three noses breathing down his neck. A car or truck in the paddock is cause for investigation. Pasture and barn repairs always take longer than estimated because of the horses' curiosity.

Horses can be mischievous, too. We used to own one whose greatest pleasure was stealing a broom from the barn so that he could carry it around in his mouth. He would trot up and down our paddock shaking it just as hard as he could. Nowadays we have a small cart which we sometimes lean upside-down against the barn wall. Sam thinks it's fine sport to keep the wheels spinning. Every now and then he forgets and sticks his nose on the wheel while it's still going. His reaction and the expression on his face are wonderful. There are all kinds of stories about the silly things horses like to do.

Horses have a type of inside radar. Chances are your horse will bring you home if you find yourself lost in the woods. Some have been reported to have found their homes from a distance of twenty miles. When I was small I often went riding alone. One day, when, typical of a child, I was more interested in the sights around me than I was in where I was going, I got lost. After a moment of panic, I remembered that horses were supposed to be able to find their way home, so I turned my horse loose and hoped for the best. Jeb grazed for a short while and then started to amble. I can't say our route was the most desirable. We crashed through underbrush for what seemed like hours. But he did carry me home.

If horses are treated well, they learn to rely upon and trust those who care for them. A perfect example of this was the day many years ago when one of our two horses came down with colic. Jeb and Scott were out in pasture far from sight of the house. We would have had no knowledge of Scott's problem until evening except that Jeb started to whinny. He called and called and somehow the sound reached me. I ran to the pasture to find Scott down on the ground obviously suffering. Jeb was intermittently calling for help and kicking Scott viciously, trying to force him to his feet. As soon as I arrived and took over, Jeb stopped all his fussing. When an

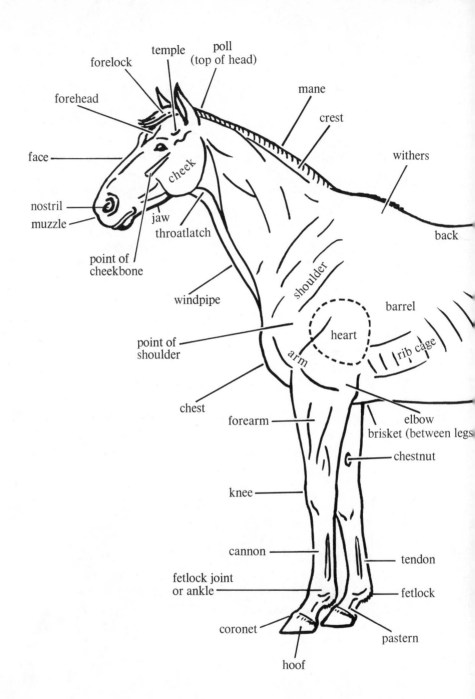

temple
poll
(top of head)
forelock
forehead
mane
crest
face
cheek
withers
nostril
jaw
muzzle
throatlatch
back
point of
cheekbone
windpipe
shoulder
barrel
point of
shoulder
heart
rib cage
arm
chest
elbow
forearm
brisket (between legs)
chestnut
knee
cannon
tendon
fetlock joint
or ankle
fetlock
coronet
pastern
hoof

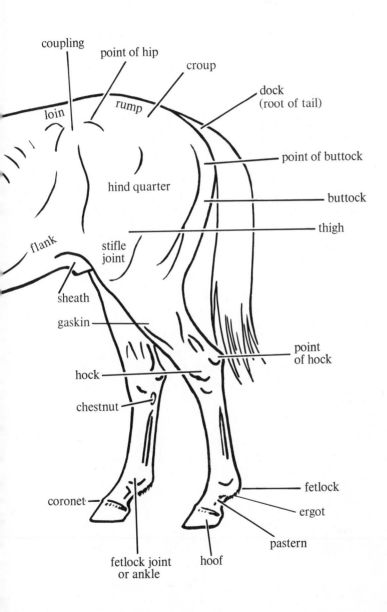

coupling

point of hip

croup

dock
(root of tail)

loin

rump

point of buttock

hind quarter

buttock

thigh

flank

stifle
joint

sheath

gaskin

point
of hock

hock

chestnut

coronet

fetlock

ergot

pastern

fetlock joint
or ankle

hoof

animal has that kind of faith in you, how can you possibly let him down? No one will ever convince me that horses aren't intelligent. In this particular situation, Jeb's thinking probably saved Scott's life.

COLOR AND MARKINGS OF THE HORSE

Being able to recognize the colors of the horse is helpful when you are describing a horse to your friends, when you are searching for lost horses, or when you are trying to buy or sell a horse. For your reference, here they are (except for "black" which obviously requires no explanation).

Bay: The color varies from light red to dark brown. Bays always have a black mane, tail, and stockings. Stockings are the markings of the leg from below the knee to the hoof. The mane, tail, and stockings are called points.

Chestnut: The color is usually a shade of red. The mane and tail are the same or a lighter color. A horse may have white on his face or his legs but he is still called a chestnut. Sometimes the very bright red color is called sorrel.

Grey: The color varies from dark steel grey to light silver grey. Most grey horses are born darker colored and later turn shades of grey and white.

Brown: The color is brown, sometimes almost black, but the horse has a lighter tan color around his eyes and muzzle. He will have black points. A dark bay and a brown horse are often confused. Many times a horse will be listed as "dark bay or brown" on his papers or on a racing form. Even the experts can't tell.

Palomino: The horse is a golden honey color with a white mane and tail.

Appaloosa: This horse is white with black or brown crazy spottings that usually have a definite pattern, i.e., spotted blanket, leopard, marble, or snowflake.

Roan: The horse has white hairs mixed with hair of some other color. The strawberry roan has white hair mixed with red. The blue roan has white hair mixed with black or brown.

Pinto: The horse has large spots of white mixed with some other color. A piebald is white and black. A skewbald is white and any color but black.

HEAD MARKINGS

Star: A white mark on the forehead.

Snip: A vertical white mark between the nostrils.

Blaze: A broad white mark on the face.

Strip: A narrow white mark from the center of the forehead to the nose.

Bald: A broad white mark that covers almost the entire head.

Two purebred horses: on the left, Son, a Thoroughbred, on the right, Sam, a Quarter Horse.

3

Buying a Horse

There are many different breeds of horses. Contrary to what many people believe, a Thoroughbred is a specific breed of horse. A horse is called a purebred, not a Thoroughbred, if he has papers which legally record his ancestry, whether the breed be Quarter Horse, Thoroughbred, Appaloosa, or Shetland Pony. A purebred horse was bred for a reason. His conformation, or physique, lends itself to certain functions. The Thoroughbred is bred for racing, show jumping, and hunting; the Standardbred for trotting; and so on.

There are also mixed breed horses. Similar to mutts, they have no papers and obviously are not considered purebred. The mixed breed horse is bred principally for pleasure.

My personal opinion is that the average stable owner should NOT buy a purebred horse of any kind. Generally they tend to be more nervous and excitable than the mixed breed horse. Usually they cost a great deal more money, too, because you are paying not only for the horse itself but for the thought and care that went into breeding. A half-bred or mixed breed horse can be a delight to own. They often have many of the qualities of the purebred, but are not nearly as sensitive. They will forgive your mistakes much more readily and they adapt more quickly to the informal atmosphere of a family stable.

All horses, mixed or purebred, have different qualities. Think very carefully before deciding exactly why you want to buy a horse. Ask yourself a number of questions.

—Who is going to ride the horse? The whole family? One small child? One large child? The entire neighborhood?

—Where do you plan to ride the horse? Is he to be ridden principally on trails, in the back pasture, or at a riding arena?

—What purpose have you in mind for the horse? Is he strictly for pleasure, for work, for jumping, for showing, for hunting?

—What kind of rider is the person who will be riding the horse?

More bones have been broken and confidences shattered than you can imagine by well-meaning people who have put beginners on excitable mounts. A beginning rider does not need a prancing, dancing Man o' War. He needs a quiet, peaceful soul who will be more than willing to go where the beginner wishes to go with a minimum of trouble. Be fair and honest with yourself. Riding pleasure will be increased tenfold when the rider is on a suitable horse.

In simple language, and I am very serious about this, a beginner is a person who can walk, trot, and perhaps canter with a minimum of security and much flapping of arms and legs. A novice rider can walk, trot, canter, and gallop (fast canter) with reasonable dexterity . . . *if* he is on a reliable horse. An intermediate rider can do all the above, jump at least three feet in good form, and is not frightened if his horse bounces around a bit. Judge accordingly, and look for the horse who fits your needs.

As your ability to ride and care for a horse increases, perhaps you'll wish to buy a purebred, although even some advanced riders don't ever want to be bothered with one. But *don't* buy one just to parade him and his pedigree in front of your friends. It may sound impressive, but when your purebred horse seriously hurts someone because of your inexperi-

A beginner doesn't belong on a prancing, dancing Man o' War.

ence, he will no longer seem so pretty and showy. You will have ruined the potential of a fine horse and given him a bad reputation to boot. Most behavior faults of the horse are the result of a poor or unknowledgeable rider. Give yourself a chance to learn.

Buying a horse is not difficult. There are many available. Buying the horse who is right for you is very difficult. The best advice I can give is to tell you to visit a reputable dealer. We've all heard jokes about horse traders and their shady deals. Shady deals do happen all the time. However, the good horse dealer takes pride in finding the kind of horse you should have for the type of riding you want to do. Rely on his judgment. Finding the right horse is how he builds his reputation and, naturally, a good reputation results in more business.

If you don't know of a reputable dealer, go shopping. Visit some of the riding stables in your area. Compare the cleanliness of the stables and the health of the horses in each. Look for horses with bright eyes and glossy coats. I don't mean necessarily that they have to be spotlessly clean, but they should give the illusion of health. A clean stable will not smell rancid, aisles will be swept, and utensils and feed bins will be neat and orderly. Almost all stables will be connected with or know of a person who buys and sells horses. Speak with the people you meet in the nicer stables. Ask whom they would recommend as a good, trustworthy dealer. One or two names will come to the fore.

Of course, dealers can and do make mistakes. Even the most honest dealer can get the wrong impression of the type of animal you want, and the horse he selects for you could turn out to be different from what he had expected. Well-meaning friends often make more mistakes. Deals with friends can be unfortunate, especially if the horse doesn't work out well for you. You, the buyer, are ashamed to admit your error. Your friend, the seller, feels guilty for not steering you in the right direction, or even worse, becomes angry because you don't like his horse. "The horse always went beautifully for me," he thinks. By buying through a dealer you avoid the possibility of a scarred friendship. Many horses are bought through friends, newspapers, and other media and these sales can be successful, but you had better know exactly what you are looking for, and most people don't. Those who do are the exception not the rule.

Once you have found a horse you think suits your specific requirements, watch him carefully. Owning a horse is a personal experience. The blending of your personality and the horse's has everything to do with your acceptance of a horse as your own. Look to see if his ears stay forward as you approach him or if they go way back indicating his possible dislike for people. Does he try to bite you? Is he willing to stand while you walk around him or does he kick out or prance around? No doubt you will be the one caring for him. Even if you stable him elsewhere, there will be times when you must work with him. It's no fun to be caught in a stall with a horse who is trying to trample you or who likes to bite or crowd you. If the horse is to be used by or around children, check to see if loud noises or waving arms frighten him unduly. If they do, nice as he might be, that horse is obviously not for you. Lead him to see if he follows you willingly.

By all means try to arrange to keep the horse for a week or two in your own stable. If this is not possible, ride the horse several times both with and without company. This way you will soon have a fair idea of the horse's personality and his willingness to go along with your wishes. Some vices can be cured. A horse who is reluctant to leave the stable, for instance, can be taught the confidence to leave happily. Other vices can be more of a problem. A horse with the habit of rearing, for example, could be much more difficult to train and might be dangerous. Don't take a problem of this kind upon yourself unless you are an experienced horseman or have the advice of one nearby. Find the horse with good manners to begin with.

Please buy a horse who looks as if he fits his intended rider. A tall man looks ridiculous on a small horse even if the horse is well-muscled and wide enough to carry him. A tiny child will have a terrible time trying to get his legs around a big horse no matter how kind and gentle the horse seems to be. Even a "pushbutton" horse has to have a rider on him large enough to reach the right buttons.

Owning a horse is a personal experience.

Give some thought to the color of the horse you buy. Greys, for instance, are very pretty to look at, but they are light in color and therefore more difficult to clean. Ours is a family stable. We try to keep our horses reasonably well groomed not only because it is good conditioning for them but because we like them to look good. But our grey, Pushover, does try my patience. Some horses stay clean and some stay dirty. I'm firmly convinced Push likes to be dirty. If he weren't so kind and so reliable I'd get rid of him tomorrow. But he's a grand horse so we keep him and suffer.

Bays and chestnuts obviously will not show the dirt and manure stains as much as the lighter grey, palomino, pinto, or roan might. White head markings and stockings are flashy and pretty to look at but they get dirty, too.

There is an old saying:

> One white leg, buy him,
> Two white legs, try him,
> Three white legs, deny him,
> Four white legs, cut him up
>   and feed him to the crows.

Don't believe a word of it. It's just an old wives' tale, probably made up by someone who was sick and tired of cleaning his horse's legs.

Actually, there has been a great deal of discussion on this subject among horsemen. Some maintain that the lighter pigmentation on a horse's leg is a sign that there is weakness in that leg. To the best of my knowledge there has never been any real proof of this. I've seen some fine horses go on and on for years with three or four white socks.

When you are satisfied that you have really found the right horse for you, have him looked over by a reputable veterinarian. You can find him the same way you found your dealer. Having a horse vetted is terribly important. Far better you lose a few dollars in the beginning to find out before you buy whether he is sound in leg and healthy, than three months later find yourself with a lame or sick horse who is no good to you or anyone else.

Sam finding the only mud in the pasture.

Unfortunately, you could end up with a sick horse anyway. We have friends who were extremely careful when buying a horse. They found a lovely one through an excellent dealer. The horse was vetted thoroughly and was pronounced well in every way. A few months later, the horse dropped dead. To the best of my knowledge, no one knows why. Realize that although this situation is rare, it can happen. At that point the only thing to do is to throw up your hands and say, "Well, that's horses!" A good veterinarian and a good dealer do the best they can. But horses don't talk.

Let me state my definition of a successful horse buy: When a horse can be bought and enjoyed not just for one year but over a period of years; when a horse because of your care and training either learns good performance and manners or keeps the fine manners and performance he had initially; when your horse, if you outgrow him in size or talent, can be sold as a horse of which you can be proud, then, you have made a successful buy.

I have purposely refrained from stating costs. Prices will vary depending upon the section of the country you live in, the time of year you wish to buy, and the type of riding you want to do. The only thing I can tell you is that, just as in buying a car or a house, you usually end up spending more than you anticipated.

Give a great deal of thought to obtaining some additional insurance when you buy a horse. Just in case, despite all of your efforts, your horse takes it upon himself to roam. You will lose your neighbors' friendship very quickly if their well-manicured lawns are torn up by horses' feet, or their valuable gardens or farms are damaged. The horse-owner may even be held responsible if his horse hits a car.

A three-horse stable with adjoining storage space.

4

Stabling

Unfortunately, many of us can't build the ideal stable. Usually we happen to have a little something out back that, with a little fixing up, might fit a horse or two. There is nothing wrong with that premise. Go ahead and use whatever you have available. But do please follow a few important principles to insure the health and comfort of your horse. If you can't incorporate the necessary features into your barn, wait until you can before putting a horse into it.

A stable should be well ventilated. A cold barn in which air can circulate is far better for your horse than an airtight stuffy barn with a window blowing air directly on him. Horses who stand in direct drafts can catch cold. Windows in stalls should always be covered with wire mesh or some other suitable material to keep horses and glass away from each other. A heated barn is not necessary. Horses gain warmth from one another during the winter months. Blankets can be used for extra warmth. Extreme changes in temperature (i.e., hot indoors, freezing out-of-doors) also leave horses susceptible to colds.

The ceiling of the stable should be high. Even the best mannered of horses will become frightened at times. The horse should be able to swing or raise his head without striking it on the ceiling. Nine feet is a good starting height for the average horse.

Electricity is helpful. Light of some sort is necessary. Especially since your horse might decide to get sick in the middle of the night. A vet will not appreciate trying to peer at him by means of a flashlight. A dark winter day isn't the easiest thing for a blacksmith to shoe by either. You might wish to show or hunt your horse. That always includes a night visit to the barn. Oil lanterns and the like do provide light, but they may cause a fire. Any fire in a barn is dangerous. Horses can panic, and they can often be so frightened that they will refuse to leave the barn.

Keep lights far away from your horse's head. See that the sockets and fixtures are not within touching distance. A shock on the hind end could be rather disturbing. Also, horses like to play with electrical switches. A friend tells the story about a horse who scared the wits out of her one very dark night by consistently turning the lights on and off in the stable. Burglars and prowlers came to mind. Who would have thought it was only one of her horses amusing himself.

Keep electrical wires in good condition. Check often to see that they are not frayed. Most stable fires today are caused by faulty wiring.

Stalls and stall doors should be large. A box stall should be at least 12 feet by 12 feet to accommodate the average 15-hand horse. The door should be at least 4 feet wide. A straight stall should be at least 6 feet by 10 feet. If at all possible, give your horse a box stall. Every horse, if he has the choice, will lie down to sleep. But the stall must be big enough. A horse can get cast, or stuck, in a stall that is so small that he doesn't have room to get up again.

The sides of the stall should be solid. They should be at least chest high to your horse and sturdy by a horse's standard, not yours. See that there

A box stall.

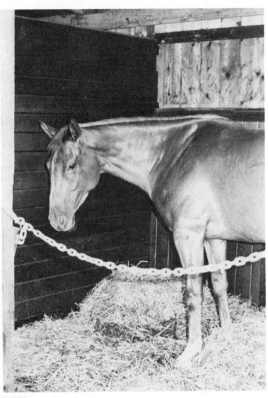

Pushover in a straight stall.

are no openings near his feet. Horses have a genuine talent for getting their feet caught between lower boards in a stall. Or, for that matter, in a pasture fence.

Stalls should have smooth sides. Whether you have a box stall or a straight stall, make sure there are no protruding nails, wood, or other jagged edges that your horse could scrape himself on. Don't forget to include the ceiling while you are checking. This is only common sense, but it is too seldom thought about.

Put a proper lock on the stall door. Horses are quite good at figuring out how to unlock doors. Make sure the latch of the adjoining stall is out of reach, too. If a horse can't reach his own latch, he'll be more than happy to accommodate his pal in the next stall. Be sure to put good locks on pasture gates too.

Make some sort of sturdy divider to separate the upper parts of the stalls. If you have more than one horse, a divider made of iron grating or slats of wood will help. Almost anything will do. Horses need company and should be able to see one another, but they do tend to fight, especially at feeding time. The bites and bruises that result are not worth having if they can be avoided.

Don't put a drain directly in the middle of a stall. Inevitably a drain placed in the center of a stall will get clogged with bedding and other material and be difficult to repair. However, a drain placed under a porous floor is acceptable if the drain is properly tiled. Otherwise, a tiled drain off to the side with an immediate outlet to the outside is best.

Keep the drawbacks of your particular stable in mind and care for your horse accordingly. For example, consider the flooring. A person walking downtown on hard sidewalks often suffers from sore feet and legs when he gets home. There is no resiliency in the pavement. A horse will suffer from a non-resilient floor in the same way.

Sides of stalls and stall doors should be solid and chest-high.

A clay floor is the best flooring for the horse because it is non-porous but resilient. Less bedding is necessary because it is soft. If the floor is set at a very slight angle with some form of drain, you will have the stall that is easier to clean.

A wood plank floor is relatively soft for a horse to stand on but it retains the smell of urine, is noisy, and needs to be kept extra clean. It must be checked regularly for rotting. Creosote or other wood protection helps, but count on replacing the floor from time to time.

A cement floor is terribly hard. A horse standing on cement for long periods of time will be very uncomfortable and can eventually become lame. However, a cement floor is probably the easiest to clean and is certainly long-lasting. A large advantage is that it can be hosed down. Horses who are out in pasture most of the time will not be hurt by a cement floor as long as you provide plenty of bedding while they are in.

Store feed in an out-of-the-way place. Stepping over bags of grain every time you enter a stable is annoying. If you are fortunate enough to have a separate room in your barn, keep the feed there along with other stable items.

Store bedding and hay in a clean and dry place. Have enough room for both. A horse will probably consume at least two-thirds of a bale of hay a day. The amount of bedding depends, of course, on the type of floor you have.

Don't ignore bedding. It is used to absorb moisture, to provide warmth, and to serve as padding for a horse's legs. There are many kinds to choose from. The most common throughout the country are straw, servel, peat moss, and wood shavings and/or sawdust.

Straw should be clean, dry, and free from mold. Oat and wheat straw are the two most commonly used. Oat straw is more palatable, and thus more likely to be eaten, so it is better to use wheat straw. Unfortunately there are some horses, our Sam included, who like to eat even wheat straw

Store bedding and hay in a clean, dry place.

and manage to finish up their bedding every night. This plays havoc with a horse's proper feeding schedule and is most unsanitary. In some parts of the country straw has become very expensive. In either case you may wish to look for another more suitable type of bedding.

Servel is composed mostly of crushed sugarcane. It is not palatable and comes packaged, which makes it easy to store. However, it is usually lumpy and has to be broken up when spread in a stall. It can be dusty.

Peat moss is, of course, soft and porous. It does retain odor, however, and is heavy to clean when it gets packed with manure and urine.

If you live near a saw mill you are in luck. To me, a mixture of wood shavings and sawdust is the greatest boon to the horse-owner. It absorbs most stable odors, and is light in color and weight, which makes a stall very

Once a cowbarn, this is now a home for our three horses.

easy to clean. However, storage is a problem and sawdust can be dusty. If you do use wood shavings make sure to check for sharp pieces of wood or other things that might injure a horse.

Remember . . . the harder the floor, the more bedding necessary to protect the horse.

See that the bedding is neither musty nor dusty, whatever kind you decide upon. We're all well enough aware of pollution these days to know how uncomfortable it is to live in a smoggy or dusty atmosphere. Animals react badly to this atmosphere, too. They get allergies and lung diseases just as humans do. If your horse must be inside all the time except for exercise, dusty wood shavings are not for him. If he comes in only to sleep or when the weather is bad, servel or wood shavings are easier to handle than straw and probably won't hurt him.

Keep the stalls clean. Some people prefer to fill up a stall with a large amount of clean bedding, and then during the week remove the worst of the manure and urine. Then on the weekend they clean out the entire stall, let it air, and fill it up again for the week to come. Another procedure is to heap clean bedding on top of the old. Each sounds like a lot of work to me. I would rather muck out the soiled areas and sweep clean every day. The time involved is short because the soiled areas are smaller, the

Here a garage has been made over into a home for one horse, with storage space above.

stalls stay cleaner, the stable smells better and I've saved myself or my family from a long, tiring weekend job.

Manure is a problem. A large pile is unpleasant to look at and extremely unpleasant to smell, and it attracts all sorts of annoying bugs. Some stable owners contract with nurseries to have it hauled away. Others put an ad in a country paper when the pile gets big enough. Usually you can find a farmer who will take it to spread on his fields. If you have enough fields of your own, you can make good use of it yourself. Don't spread new manure where you expect your horses to graze. It must age or the grass will grow in sour and the horses will refuse to eat it. Wait a few weeks at least. Longer is preferable. Straw and peat moss refuse will decompose much more quickly than sawdust.

5

Feeding

Feeding a horse a well-balanced diet each day is very important. Many studies have been made to determine the proper nutritional values for maintaining a manageable but high performance horse. Racehorse-owners, breeding stables, and large horse-feed companies are among the groups looking for the perfect grass, the perfect vitamin supplement, and so on.

Although we know that every horse is particular unto himself and that some may require a different or even an unusual diet, most horse diets can follow a general rule of thumb. Of course, every horse-owner should take his own horse into consideration and use the guidelines with care.

A horse's stomach is very small compared to the size of his body. As a result, a little feed at a time is all he can handle without making himself sick. A horse out on pasture slowly munches away at grass and other forage all day. Obviously, a horse who is on pasture does not need as much grain feed as the horse who lives indoors and relies on us for all his food.

All horses need:

> An energy food (grain)
> A food with laxative qualities

A food to give bulk (hay, grass, etc.)
Water
Salt

The most common energy foods today are oats, sweet feed, and pellets. Oats provide a lot of protein along with other nutrients and are the most favored of the grain feeds. They can be given whole, rolled, or coarsely ground. A good, clean, crimped (or pressed) oat is probably the best—more nutritious feed can be given at one time because the outer shell is crushed. You've heard the saying "he's feeling his oats" applied to a high-spirited youngster. Give a horse too many oats and you'll know why someone thought it up.

Sweet feed, usually a prepared horse feed, is principally a mixture of oats, corn, and molasses. There are several brands available or you can mix your own with a veterinarian's advice. Corn is a real supplier of heat. Molasses is tasty and a carbohydrate. Sweet feed is a rich diet, however, and must be given carefully. Every horse responds to it differently.

Pellets are another prepared horse feed. They are relatively new to the horse world and were devised to put all the nutrients for a complete horse diet into one food. They help solve the difficult problem of finding hay in some parts of the country, because forage is included in the feed. Personally, I find pellets the greatest thing in the world. Our horses have hunted quite successfully off of them and yet, if there is a time when the family is too busy to ride, we can return to our horses later to find them still fit but amenable to our wishes.

Bran's principal use today is as a laxative. It is easily digested and is often fed as a companion to oats. Some horsemen prefer to feed only oats or sweet feed and then once a week combine two to four quarts of bran with enough hot water to make a mash. Mixed with a little salt and then cooled to eating temperature, a bran mash makes the best-smelling concoction you could imagine and most horses love it. Whether you feed your

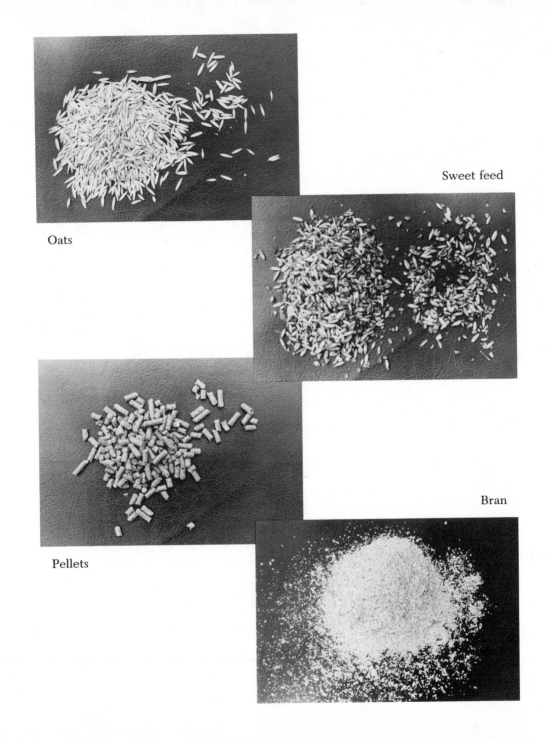

Oats

Sweet feed

Pellets

Bran

horse a mash or a small dry cupful of bran with the oats at each feeding doesn't matter. What does matter is that the horse be supplied with a laxative at some time.

As a rule, if you feed your horse pellets you do not need bran, as that is included in the feed. Many horsemen, yours truly included, prefer to feed a smaller ration of pellets than the directions suggest and continue to supply hay. The major reason for this is that horses who stand in a stall all day with nothing to do become bored. When horses are bored they can pick up all sorts of bad stable habits. They may start to pace in their stalls. They may start to chew on the sides of their stalls. They may begin to weave their heads back and forth. They may start kicking. Who knows what they may think of. The unfortunate thing is that once a horse develops a bad habit, or vice as it is sometimes called, it is very difficult and sometimes impossible to rid him of it.

Hay is the most common roughage. A good hay provides bulk, energy, vitamins, minerals, and proteins. Hay is cut, then made into sections. A series of sections are placed together forming a bale, which facilitates delivery and storage. A wire-tied bale is packed more tightly and therefore has more body than the loosely-tied twine bale.

Timothy hay is often preferred because it is cleaner than some of the other types of hay. Alfalfa is more nourishing but because it is rich, a smaller portion should be given. A good mixture of four parts timothy and two parts alfalfa or clover is ideal. Horsemen seem to disagree as to when hay should be bought. Some claim the first cutting has the highest food value. Others claim the second or third cutting is better. The only conclusion I can come to is that it will probably depend upon the climate and soil in your part of the country. Try a bale or two from each cutting and see which one your horse likes to eat and seems to thrive on. Don't look for inferior hay in an attempt to save money. You've defeated your purpose anyway if the horse needs a great deal of hay to get the nourishment he needs. Pay a little more and give him less.

Water is as necessary for your horse as it is for you. The only danger

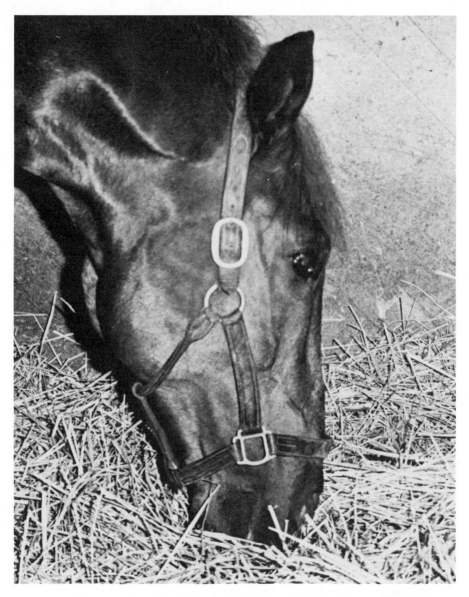

Hay may be placed on the floor if you keep a clean stall.

involved is in providing too much of it after your horse has been worked heavily. A hot, overtired horse can get very sick if he drinks too much. Water should always be available, otherwise, and it should be clean.

All animals need salt. Place a large block of it out in the pasture so that your horses can help themselves, or keep a small block available in each stall. It can be placed right in the feed box. Summer is obviously the most important time to supply salt, although it should be available at all times of the year. If you do keep a block out in the pasture you will probably discover that your horses have had visitors. Deer and other wild animals love it and will help themselves.

When the vet checks your horse for soundness, have him suggest a proper diet. *You are doing neither yourself nor your horse a kindness by overfeeding him.* Most horses will be very happy with far less than you might believe. An overfed horse is usually packed so full of vitamins and other energy foods that he can hardly contain himself. He is even less fun to ride. A fat horse is no healthier than a fat person. Don't feel that he must have large portions of grain just because everyone else seems to be feeding large portions. They could be wrong. Feel free to experiment but use common sense. A safe rule to follow is to feed your horse the smallest portion you can. If he stays round and healthy, why feed him more? If he starts to lose weight, acts sluggish or tired, increase the feed until he looks good and rides well for you again. Naturally, a horse working hard day in and day out will need much more feed than a horse who goes out once or twice a week.

There are two good starter diets for the average family horse who is not working long hours each day. One is two or three pounds of good horse pellets a day and some hay. Another is two to four pounds of oats each time you feed, with a cupful of bran and some hay. We use the 1 quart 14 oz. juice can to measure our feed. The can will hold about 1¾ lbs. of small-sized pellets or 1½ lb. of crushed oats. Almost every town has a feed and grain store nearby in which to buy grain and even hay and straw. However, most horsemen prefer to deal directly with the farmer when buying hay and straw. This way they can buy in bulk and save a good bit of money.

A pony needs very little grain. Reduce the amount of feed in proportion to the size of the animal. A cup of pellets and a section of hay morning and night should suffice.

Grain feed is normally given morning and night. It is better to give hay before the grain as it takes the edge off the horse's appetite and not so much grain is wasted. Horses often have a tendency to throw their grain around in their eagerness to eat it. If a horse or pony is not out on pasture and cannot benefit from grass, or if the pasture is small, two sections of hay should be given at least morning, noon, and night to compensate for what he is missing in pasture. Otherwise, two sections morning and night should be sufficient. If the grass is really rich, and you can tell that by the speed with which your horse starts to put on weight, even less hay and grain are necessary. Don't give your horse more hay than he will eat. It is wasteful and, of course, unsanitary if he tramples all over it.

If your horse is working very hard, day after day, break up the large amount of feed he requires by feeding him at least three times a day. There are many horsemen who feed their horses five times a day.

Don't ride a horse directly after he has eaten. It takes him at least an hour and a half to properly digest his food. Ride him any earlier and you take the risk of making him quite sick.

An ideal arrangement: feedbox, bucket of clean water, hay on floor, stall with sturdy sides, chest-high, and bars above to separate the horse from his neighbor.

6

Basic
Stable Equipment

There are many items of stable equipment for you to think about. First consider the stall accessories. You will need a *feed box* or some kind of holder in which to put your horse's feed. Iron is probably your best bet because it is sturdy, although a wood box is most acceptable. If you use a wood box, line it with metal to protect it from wearing thin over a period of time. If it's not possible for you to arrange for either one, there are some wonderful plastic feeders on the market that make good substitutes. Do make your feeder stationary for the eating period and keep it away from the floor. The feeder should be kept clean.

There should be some sort of *apparatus for water.* All horses should be free to drink whenever they wish unless they are overheated. The ideal is an automatic water fountain. Whenever your horse wants to drink, he presses the paddle of the fountain and water runs out. If it's impossible to have a fountain, buckets again will do the trick. Try to keep the water bucket away from the area where the horse eats his hay and grain. Hauling water is a chore anyway, and if his feed is nearby, a horse will often drop half of it into the water just for fun. We have a new horse who likes to do this. He makes constant trips from one end of the stall to the other. My

Automatic water fountain.

Hayrack.

only satisfaction comes from knowing that he is dropping most of the grain before he gets to the water. We're hoping he'll discover it's a waste of time and will forget the whole thing. Clean water receptacles are essential.

I don't believe it's necessary for a horse to have a hay rack. Hay can be dropped on the floor if you keep a reasonably clean stall. Many horsemen feel that hay should be given in this fashion, as it is natural for a horse's head to be down as he grazes. Other horsemen prefer to place the hay in a rack above the ground, as it guarantees that the hay will stay clean. If you use a rack, be careful about its placement. Place it too high and dust and seeds can fall into the horse's eyes. Place it too low and most likely the horse will catch his feet between the slats.

The choice of cleaning or "mucking out" tools depends upon the kind of bedding you use. A good *broom* is a necessity. A *pitchfork* is used to carry hay and also to clean a straw stall. We have discovered that a *sawed-off rake* and a *small shovel* are handiest when using servel or wood shavings. It's easy to see the soiled areas in this kind of bedding and they can be raked into the shovel in no time at all. Have a *lightweight wheelbarrow* nearby in which to load manure. The trip from the stall to the manure pile is then fairly simple, even for a child.

There are many kinds of cleaning utensils for your horse. Basically, one needs a *curry comb* to scrub the dirt loose, a *dandy brush* to get the heavy dirt off, a *body brush,* which is softer and finer, for the finishing effects, a *mane and tail comb,* and a *hoof pick* to clean the feet. Bear in mind the person who will be cleaning your horse. If it is a child, get brushes that will fit in his hands. They are available.

Additional utensils that you may want to have are a *body scraper* to get rid of excess water and snow, a *shedding blade* to get rid of excess hair in the spring, *clippers,* either electric or manual, to trim the ears, chin whiskers and legs, and, if you are very lucky, a *vacuum cleaner.* Saves lots of elbow grease.

Your horse needs a *halter,* a simple affair that slips onto his head for leading and holding purposes. There are rope halters, there are nice wash-

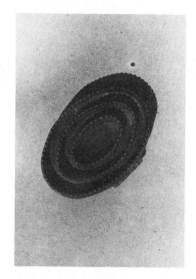

Curry comb

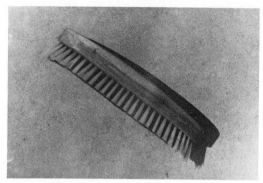

Dandy brush

Mane and tail comb

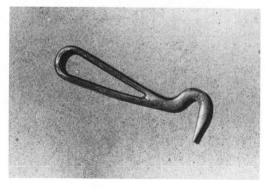

Body brush

Hoof pick

able nylon halters, and there are beautiful leather halters. Take your choice. Just remember to get your horse one that is sturdy and see that it fits comfortably. Try to avoid leaving a halter on all the time, as it can rub and cause loss of hair and possibly sores.

Rope shanks are necessary, too. A shank is a long strong rope with a snap hook on the end. When attached to the halter, it makes a nice rope for leading your horse. Stationary shanks tied to a wall on either side form a simple tie when you want your horse in a more open place for grooming or other care. There are chain shanks available too.

A large *container for feed* is good to have. Line it with sheet metal, as rats, chipmunks, and mice are notorious for breaking into feed. A latch on the container isn't a bad idea either. It should discourage your horse even if he does break out and go investigating without your knowing it. A wooden bin is pretty, but good old-fashioned 20-gallon galvanized garbage cans do nicely too.

Don't forget a *trash basket*. Stables get just as messy as any other place.

All of the equipment used on a horse is called *tack*. A *saddle and bridle rack* will help keep your saddle and bridle in good condition. There are all kinds of fancy racks to choose from or you can use your own ingenuity to devise one. A sawhorse works very well to hold a saddle, and coffee cans can be used as bridle holders.

Unless they are turned out all of the time, horses should have a *blanket* in cold weather. Blankets are usually made of heavy canvas or duck and can be wool-lined. They come in all sizes so watch out when you go to buy one. A *sheet* is a much lighter blanket used to keep your horse clean or to protect him from flies. Sheets are often used when vanning. A *cooler* is a light wool blanket used for the same purpose as an athlete would use a sweat shirt and sweat pants.

You will want to keep a few *medicines* available. PHisohex is wonderful for cleaning wounds. There are also any number of antiseptic powders and liquids. Vaseline is used to keep wounds clean and to prevent loss of hair. You should have as many bandages as you have horse's legs. Cotton

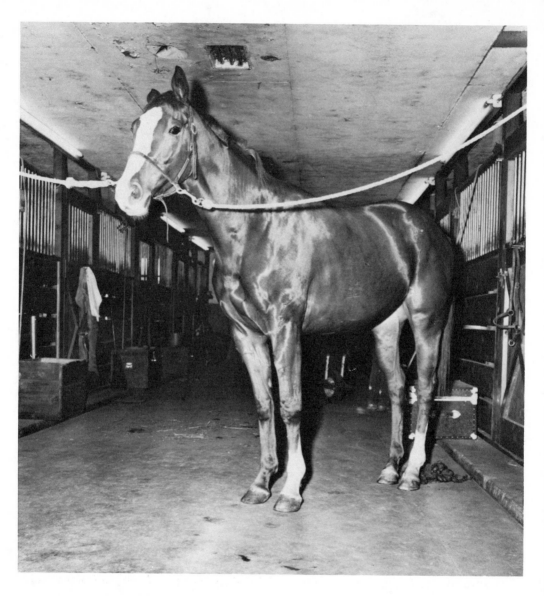

Shanks secured to a wall on either side make a good tie when you want your horse in the open for grooming and other care.

Please keep your saddle on a rack. Here is one of the many kinds available.

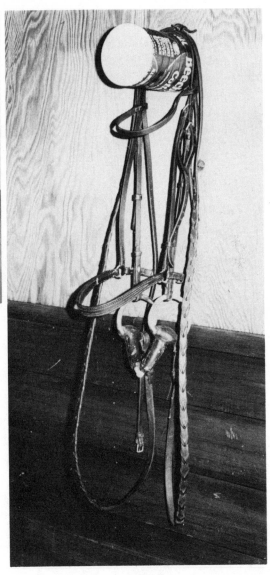

Even a coffee can may be used as a bridle holder.

squares large enough to go around the horse's leg are sometimes placed under the bandage. A good fly spray or solution will protect your horse in warm weather. Liniment is needed for sore and aching muscles. Worm medicine is easily acquired if you want it; the same goes for colic medicine. Get your vet's advice. Clean cloths and towels always come in handy. So do sponges. Your list will grow as the weeks go by.

Wearing a halter and a sheet.

7

Pasture

Every horse needs a pasture or at least some place where he can be turned out to kick up his heels and stretch his legs. If you have the space to let him out, for heaven's sake, do it. As long as a horse is allowed to get acclimated slowly to the weather and surroundings, he will prefer to be outside. And that way, the stable owner will save himself a great deal of work.

Be very careful if your horse has not been an outdoor horse. The horse unfamiliar with a pasture must be watched closely. If he eats too much rich grass when he's not used to it, he may get sick. Introduce him to it slowly, no longer than an hour at first, and watch his droppings to see that he doesn't get diarrhea. Uneven or rough pasture could cause scratches and leg problems until he becomes familiar with the footing and learns how to move over it. Cold weather can cause problems, too. Horses will naturally grow a thicker coat if they are in a cold climate. However, the thickness of the coat does not necessarily reflect the amount of insulation the horse may have against the cold and wet. A horse whose winter coat is really working has a natural tendency to repel rain and snow. Another horse may have the thickness but not the undercoat to withstand the weather.

Our Sam was accustomed to spending his winters in the South. His first winter with us was difficult for him and for us because his body had not yet adjusted to the cold. We had to watch him carefully for the shivering and shaking that would inevitably occur if we erred and left him out too long. Another horse I had occasion to know and ride was not too familiar with snow. He seemed to hate it and did his best to tiptoe through it. A very strange sensation when riding him. His caretaker arrived at the pasture one cold winter's day to find him standing on his hind legs with his two front feet perched on the top rail of the fence. At least he'd figured out how to get two of his feet out of the snow. Of course, with time, both horses have learned how to get along in our climate and now do beautifully.

Our horses prefer to stay outside even in the dead of winter. If we felt sorry for them and kept them in, they would bang on their stalls with impatience. We settled the problem by letting them tell us when they wanted to come in. In very high winds, severe sleet or electrical storms, they have gathered at the barn door and have even called to us. We do insist upon bringing them in at night in the winter. We reverse the procedure in the summer. We keep them in during the day when the flies are bad and put them out at night to wander and graze in peace.

One word of warning. If you have a fondness for certain trees on your property, pad and cover the bark well. Horses love to nibble on the bark and roots of trees and will strip and kill every one if they are not protected. There are some trees that are very dangerous to horses. Wild cherry can be toxic; too many apples or other fruits could cause a severe case of colic.

If you are fortunate enough to have a barn and pasture that your horse can wander in and out of without your assistence, you can save yourself a lot of time and trouble. But here again, beware. A horse's natural curiosity could be his undoing. Take pains to see that everything is under lock and key. Too much feed will make him sick. Bottles can be broken. Tools can fall and cause panic or injury. The barn must be horse-proofed. Horse-proof the pasture, too. Check periodically for nails, glass, old wire, or

Our mulberry tree with even the roots exposed. We tried everything to protect this tree, but the horses beat us every time.

Split-rail fencing is always popular.

broken fencing. If you don't get rid of them, I guarantee your horse will find them and hurt himself. They always do.

There are many varieties of fencing available. The split rail or some other type of wood fence is always attractive and when treated for weather, usually sufficient. However, some horses deem them "jump-able." Wire mesh fencing works well for many horses and so does electric fencing. Barbed wire should be avoided as a horse could become entangled in it and really hurt himself. If you do decide to use any form of wire, hang strips of material or other vivid objects on it so the horse knows the fence is there. If the pasture is not particularly large it never hurts to walk or slowly ride him around the perimeter. Horses respect electric fencing once they have been introduced to it, and most won't go near it after the first or second shock.

Any fencing will do as long as you supply your horse with ample room to forage, run, and drink. The generally accepted rule is that a pasture should allow at least one acre per horse. Remember, too, that horses prefer to be together. One lone horse, because he's bored, may break the fence or jump out in order to find himself a friend.

Watch your horses carefully in the pasture if they are new to each other. They *will* fight. Often it is better to keep a newcomer in his stall or a separate paddock for a few days until the horses become more accustomed to one another. Our Thoroughbred, Son of Junior, gave us several real scares when we first brought him home. He wanted so badly to be in the same pasture with the other horses; but every time we tried to put them together he was literally almost killed. So back he'd go by himself again. Three weeks went by and the situation hadn't changed a bit. Then one day my husband and I arrived home from a shopping expedition to find all the horses together. Son had jumped a four-and-a-half-foot fence to get into the paddock with horses he knew would hurt him. And they did. But while we were gone, they must have had a little discussion, too, because they have been together ever since and no more near disasters have occurred.

If the pasture area is too small to supply adequate forage, your horse may try to find greener pastures. Prevent his urge to wander by supplying him with one or two sections of hay off and on throughout the day. It will keep him busy and satisfied. If you have more than one horse, place a few individual piles on the ground. Otherwise, the leader will eat it all and leave the others nothing. Make sure the piles are far enough apart so that the horses cannot make contact if they kick at one another, and if the pasture is rough (i.e., contains trees and bushes), make sure that each pile is out far enough in the open to allow each horse an escape route. Our horses continually play "ring around the rosy" when the hay is set out. Pushover is the leader. He eats from one pile, then shifts to another, then another. Sam and Son have learned to switch at Push's will. It was difficult for Son when he first arrived. Even after they were all in the same pasture both Sam and Push would chase him away from whichever pile he happened to be eating. Time eventually solved the problem, but we did give Son a good bit more hay when he was in his stall to compensate for what he was missing outside.

A word of warning about tethering. Although some horses have learned to tether successfully, most have not. We have friends who made the mistake of tethering their mare in the yard so she could have some good green grass. Somehow or other, she got tangled in the chain and the result was a horse with a broken leg. She had to be destroyed. If you do tether your horse, watch him constantly. You may save yourself a lot of grief.

8

ᴄBridle
and Saddle (Tack)

Fit tack correctly to your horse. At the least, improperly adjusted tack can upset a horse and interfere with the smoothness of his performance. A tight or twisted bridle will cause unnecessary discomfort, and an ill-fitting saddle may cause girth sores and back sores that eventually make a horse unrideable.

Correct selection of the bit can be complicated and confusing. Although bits are all designed to perform the same sort of duty, i.e., control a horse, there are many different styles depending upon the type of riding you prefer and the amount of severity the horse needs.

There is a small area about two fingers wide on each side of a horse's mouth where teeth do not grow. This area is called the bars and it is especially sensitive. Most bits are designed to rest on the bars and/or the tongue. When a rider pulls on the reins, the bit places pressure on the bars or tongue and the horse responds. If a rider pulls too hard or too suddenly, the bit causes real pain. Most horses will try to protect themselves when this occurs. Some have learned to bring their heads in almost to their chests to relieve the pressure in their mouths. Others continually shake their heads. Still others will buck, rear, lean on the bit, or in some way give

A pelham bit. The pelham, stronger than a snaffle, includes a curb chain and requires two sets of reins.

their riders a totally unpleasant ride. If a horse resists long enough his mouth sometimes becomes partially inured to the pressure. Then the rider must resort to a heavier, more severe bit to make the horse respond.

A truly fine and sensitive horseman can ride most horses with a harsh bit and never hurt them. Because his hands are so light, exerting the slightest amount of pressure only when necessary, the horses react by moving quietly and peacefully.

But the average rider, and that means most of us, has not yet achieved that finesse with his hands. He needs as much help as possible from the bridle and bit. Initially he should try to find the horse who requires the least amount of bitting but still is easy to handle. Then strong rein control is not needed nearly so often. The horse who is sensitive to commands responds readily and, therefore, is fairly well protected from his rider's inexperience.

If the horse is new or unfamiliar, find out from the past owner what kind of bridle was used. Ask if the horse seemed happy with that particular bridle. Usually you can tell yourself simply by watching the horse move under saddle. If he persists in shaking his head up and down, or appears to be difficult to stop, or in any way seems not to be holding his head quietly in a normal, alert position, you may have a problem.

Experimenting with different bridles is the obvious solution. Your saddlery shop can advise you; so can a good professional horseman. If possible, borrow a variety of bridles from your friends. Beware the horseman who claims that one particular bridle is the answer to every problem. We all have bridle preferences but, as I said before, every horse is different.

The snaffle is the softest and kindest bit. It is one piece of metal or rubber, although it may be hinged in the middle, and only the tongue and possibly the corners of the mouth are affected when the rider pulls the one set of reins. However, many horses, because of poor training, will respond only to a stronger bit. Then you need a curb, which consists of a stronger bit and a strip of chain or leather placed under the chin. With the added curb, a pull on the reins exerts pressure not only on the tongue but on the bars. At the same time, the chain or strap applies pressure on the chin groove. A straight curb bit is the softest of the curbs because the tongue acts as a slight buffer. If the bit has a port, a curve in the center of the bit, it will curve around the tongue and more pressure will be placed on the bars. More than one set of reins is sometimes needed to help control the horse as the bit becomes more complicated. On a Pelham bridle, for instance, the snaffle rein remains to do the ordinary work and a curb rein is added to make the curb bit and chain more effective when necessary.

When fitting a bridle the bit should be neither too wide so that it wiggles from side to side, nor so small that it pinches. It is placed at the proper length when each side of the horse's mouth shows no wrinkle, or one wrinkle at the most. If a curb chain is used it should rest flat in the chin groove. It should not pinch, or flap around. The noseband should drop about an inch and a half below the cheekbones and should be comfortably loose. The browband, headstall, or earstall, depending upon the make and style of bridle, should be set so that it doesn't exert much pressure on the horse's head and ears. If you have ever worn a hat that was too tight, you can understand how uncomfortable a horse might feel with a tight bridle. The throat latch, if used, is really there only as a connecting strap. It should be fairly loose, never so tight that it pinches the horse's throat and interferes with his breathing. You should be able to place three fingers comfortably under the horse's head between his throat and the latch. If you can't, it is too tight.

Getting socked in the teeth by a horse's head is no fun. A martingale is a convenient item if you have a horse with the unfortunate habit of carrying or throwing his head way up in the air. Young or untrained horses often carry their heads this way. They haven't yet figured out what the bridle is supposed to tell them.

The martingale allows a horse to keep his head in its natural position, but prevents it from going up so high that it hurts the rider. It also helps train the horse to keep his head down properly so that he, at the least, can see where he is going. It should be adjusted so that the horse can lift his

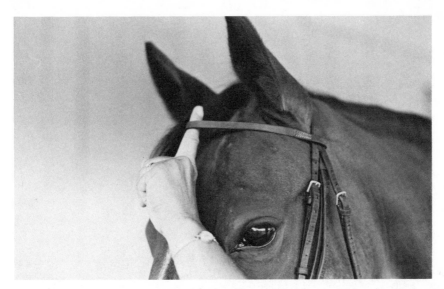

Browband properly fitted.

Throat latch properly fitted. The bridle has a snaffle bit.

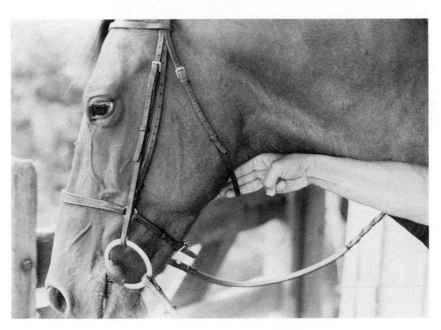

A standing martingale is by far the safest, wisest, and kindest for the average rider to use.

head high enough for his chin to be level with his withers. If it is allowed to be any looser, the martingale loses its effectiveness.

There is a running martingale which the English rider sometimes uses. However, because this martingale is attached to the reins, the rider must use much more subtle control than many people are capable of. The standing martingale is by far the safest, wisest, and kindest for the average rider to use.

What kind of saddle should you buy? Take your pick. Again the choice depends on the type of riding you prefer. Sometimes one is lucky and can find a good, well-made, second-hand saddle in a saddlery shop or through a newspaper ad. If you jump or plan to jump eventually, spend the money and invest in a forward seat saddle. This saddle has padded knee rolls to give the rider more support when he is in the forward position.

Horses fit saddles differently. A horse who has high withers or a pronounced backbone, for example, probably needs a saddle with a high throat. The saddle should fit correctly when the lowest part of the saddle remains the lowest part of the saddle when set on the horse. It should rest comfortably and evenly on his back with no apparent pressure points. You should be able to place two fingers under the pommel of the saddle at all times.

Be sure the girth or cinch is big enough to fit around the horse, as girths come in many varied lengths. A girth should be snug but not tight. The skin should be smooth, not wrinkled underneath. A 46-inch girth is usually sufficient for the average horse.

Buy a wide stirrup. If the saddle is for a child, the stirrups can be used throughout his growing years. A wide stirrup for an adult will help prevent his catching a foot in the event of a fall.

Be sure, whatever kind of saddle you buy, that *you* fit in it. After all, we come in all shapes and sizes just as the saddles do. A saddle is measured by the length of the tree, the tree being the basic structure of the saddle. The rider's height and weight play a large part in the selection because different saddles vary in the depth and width of the seat.

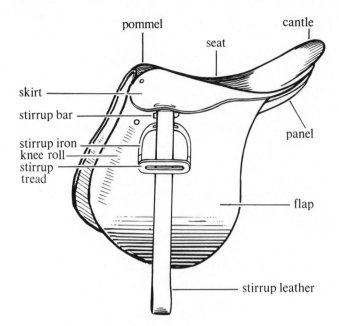

pommel

cantle

seat

skirt

stirrup bar

stirrup iron
knee roll
stirrup
tread

panel

flap

stirrup leather

ENGLISH SADDLE

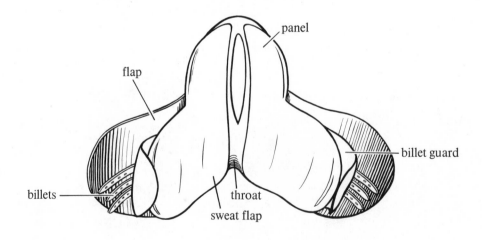

panel

flap

billet guard

billets

throat

sweat flap

ENGLISH SADDLE (UNDERSIDE)

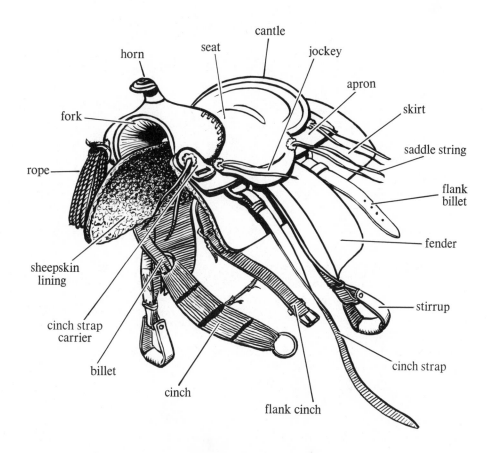

horn

fork

rope

sheepskin
lining

cinch strap
carrier

billet

cinch

flank cinch

seat

cantle

jockey

apron

skirt

saddle string

flank
billet

fender

stirrup

cinch strap

WESTERN SADDLE

Make an effort to buy a good saddle. A good saddle is expensive, but regular cleaning with saddle soap and an occasional oiling to keep it soft will make it usable and comfortable for years.

Leather need only be oiled when it begins to dry out. Don't make the mistake of oiling it too often. The constant application of oil to your tack will make it deteriorate faster. Also, the oil won't soak in completely and the result will be stained riding clothes. Instead, wash tack with saddle soap whenever it is dirty. Dry rinse and then dry well with a cloth. If you've been riding in wet weather apply any one of a number of prepared leather preservatives (they can be found in any tack shop) after cleaning to keep the leather from becoming stiff and cracked. Oil is most often used on new leather to make it soft and supple.

Leather is affected by dampness and extreme cold. If you don't have a well-protected and fairly warm area in your barn, bring your saddle to the house for protection in really cold or wet weather. Please set your saddle on some sort of rack. It would be a shame for it to be ruined be-

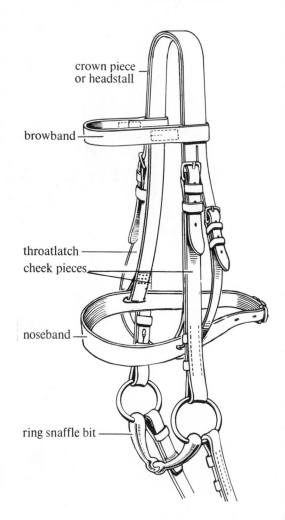

crown piece or headstall

browband

throatlatch

cheek pieces

noseband

ring snaffle bit

SNAFFLE BRIDLE

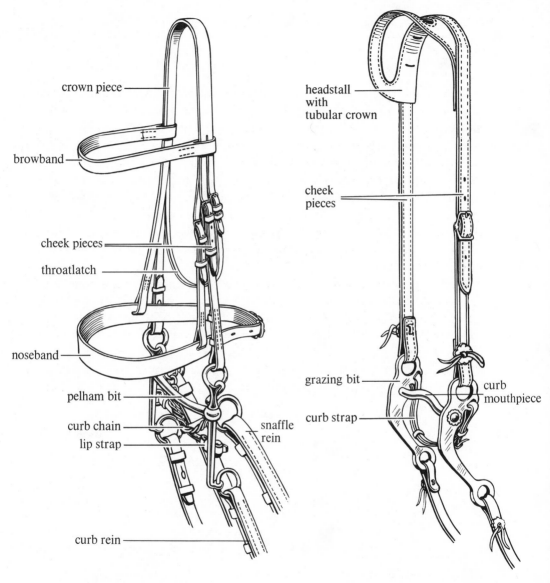

crown piece

browband

cheek pieces

throatlatch

noseband

pelham bit

curb chain

lip strap

snaffle rein

curb rein

headstall with tubular crown

cheek pieces

grazing bit

curb mouthpiece

curb strap

PELHAM BRIDLE

ONE EAR (WESTERN) BRIDLE

cause you were careless and dumped it on the floor to become misshapen and scarred.

Learn to identify the parts of the saddle and bridle. Anyone who works around horses for a while discovers that various parts of the tack eventually break or fray despite his care. Knowing the names will facilitate ordering new parts when they are needed.

Check the bridle and saddle often for defects. If you find any, have them mended at once. What a shame if you were out on a ride and suddenly found yourself with a broken rein flapping in your hand, or a girth that was no longer connected to the saddle because a billet or strap broke without your knowing it. This is not only disappointing, but dangerous. We all manage to get into enough predicaments without going out to look for them.

Unless you are absolutely certain you are correct, the less color and decoration you have on your saddle and bridle, the better dressed your horse will be. Western riders often have beautifully tooled saddles, but they are highly valued and are kept mostly for show, not for everyday riding. English riders, unless they are saddle or park seat riders, frown upon colored browbands and other fancy accoutrements. Simplicity is the key. You will be correct in any society.

9

Clothing

Riding attire is designed for the work you plan to do and is usually the most practical attire for the situation. Tradition also plays a large part.

Any comfortable old clothes will do while you're in the barn cleaning or mucking out. Parkas are excellent for the winter. They are washable, light but warm, and give you freedom to move around. Most important: your nose gets accustomed to the horsey smell, your friend's nose does not. For goodness' sake, don't put barn clothes in your closet. All of the clothes will catch the smell. Children are great offenders so watch them carefully. Keep barn coats in a separate area.

The choice of clothing becomes more important when you are going riding. Western riders usually wear blue jeans, a slim shirt, perhaps chaps, and boots with heels. The attire is worn because it is sturdy and practical for a working situation. However, riders who show or participate in rodeos often get much more fanciful and appear wearing beautifully decorated vests, long, over-the-boot pants, Western boots plain or tooled, and Western hats in whichever style the rider happens to look best. But working clothes are equally acceptable in the show ring.

Whereas the Western rider may, if he wishes, look showy and have a bit of glitter, the English rider should appear tailored, almost severe.

Reasonably formal Western attire.

Informal riding attire is very similar to the Western rider's. Stretch blue jeans for a comfortable but snug fit, a cotton shirt, and sweater are fine. For schooling sessions many riders wear jeans with chaps over them for added support. Jodhpur boots (short riding boots) or sturdy shoes with low heels are most often worn with chaps. Knee-high boots can be worn when wearing only jeans. Please don't wear sneakers. They are slippery and because they have no heel, the foot can slide completely through the stirrup and catch. Sneakers couldn't be more dangerous.

Boots for informal riding no longer need to be expensive. Saddlery shops carry high black rubber boots that look amazingly like their formal black leather counterpart. There are brown rubber boots with a canvas top called Newmarkets, and praise be, they have even come out with a sharp-looking brown rubber boot with a tan stretch top.

One should take a few more pains with his appearance for a Sunday afternoon ride in the park. Jodhpurs and jodhpur boots are acceptable. So are breeches (pronounced britches) and high boots. Colored jodhpurs are

English attire, suitable for all but the most formal occasions.

only acceptable for saddle and park seat riders. The English rider should stick to shades of tan and grey, although brown boots with brown breeches are quite nice. The shirt should be quiet in color. A man should wear a tie. A woman can have a little fun by buying an assortment of chokers. They come in all colors and are acceptable for all but the most formal riding. Although there are some very loud riding jackets on the market today, your safest bet is a tweed in muted shades. It doesn't show the dirt so quickly. The jacket must be split at the tails so you don't have to sit on it.

Hunt caps are hard hats worn by children up to the age of eighteen. They were designed for a purpose: to keep children from splitting their heads open. It will never hurt to have a child wear one. He should always wear one if he is planning to jump. This is no place to save money. Buy one no matter how much it costs.

Men and women wear derbies. The derby, too, is hard and is designed to protect the head. It has the added attraction of a brim, which comes in handy if a rider is going through brush, as it deflects the twigs that might otherwise scratch his face. The brim does a pretty fair job of keeping rain off the back of the neck, too.

Formal hunting or English show attire is a little more difficult. You will never be wrong if you wear: a hard hat, black hunt cap for juniors (up to age sixteen in the hunt field, to age eighteen in the show ring), black derby for adults; a white stock pinned with a plain gold safety pin; tan or grey breeches; black leather boots without tops (i.e., with plain tops); black or oxford grey riding jacket with plain black buttons; string gloves if you have them.

Informally, the saddle seat rider wears pretty much the same as the English rider. For show, he wears Kentucky jodhpurs, jodhpur boots, a long well-fitting riding jacket, a simple tie, white shirt, and a derby. The attire may be in color, but it is usually an all-in-one color outfit. Formally, even more conservative colors are necessary. Riders wear the tuxedo type jacket with collar and lapel of the same color, top hat and gloves.

Generally speaking, a woman's hair, no matter what style of riding, should be neatly combed and tied down so that it doesn't flap around. There is nothing more unsightly than a neat horse, a well-dressed rider, and no face—because hair is falling in front of it. Loose ponytails are not attractive either. They flop and flip. Hairnets are useful; braids carefully secured are fine.

I put chewing gum in the category of unattractiveness, too. A nicely dressed rider not only looks ridiculous but the whole picture is spoiled for the observer when the rider is chawing away on a stick of gum.

There is, as you can see, a more or less correct dress for every type of riding. Do try to follow these guidelines. Horsemen are sociable and very kind, but rarely will they tell you of the errors that you and your horse may make. Osmosis is a difficult and unsatisfactory means of learning anything. It takes far too long and the new rider is needlessly embarrassed when the fact that he has looked ridiculous finally seeps in. Attire may vary from one section of the country to another. If you are going to a new area, don't be ashamed to ask what you are expected to wear.

10

Riding Your Horse

Your style of riding will depend to some degree upon the area in which you live and the type of sport your friends prefer. The English rider rides in a flat saddle and knows how to travel cross-country, jump all kinds of fences, and even fox hunt if there is a hunt in the area. Our United States Equestrian Team rides the English seat. In the Western style of riding the saddle has a high pommel or horn in front which makes jumping an obvious danger. The saddle is designed to carry equipment, packs, ropes, cutting shears, and other necessary items for the working rider. The Western horse was trained to work with cattle and other livestock on the open range. Today he is often used for pack trips. In the show ring, the Western horse has events for cutting, bending around barrels, and generally exhibiting his perception and agility in a working situation.

The saddle or park seat rider uses a flat saddle as does the English rider. The Saddle Horse is a distinct breed, developed in the South, and formerly used by plantation owners who wanted a flashy but comfortable riding horse. Now there are other Saddle-type breeds which are offshoots of the Saddle-bred, Thoroughbred, and Morgan. All of the Saddle Horses are high-stepping prancers. They may have three gaits: walk, trot, and canter;

or they may have five gaits: walk, trot, canter, and two man-made gaits, slow gait and rack.

The dressage rider uses the flat saddle, also. Actually, dressage is controlled schooling, and it includes the high schooling of the English riding horse. The height of dressage is represented by the fabulous Lippizaner horses at the Spanish Riding School in Vienna.

All riders should be aware of the fact that a horse begins each movement with one or both of his hind legs, not the front legs as so many people believe. At the walk, a horse has a four-beat gait: hind foot, fore foot, hind foot, fore foot. When well trained, the horse should move each hind foot directly into the prints of his fore feet. The walk is brisk and straight when done correctly.

The trot is a two-beat gait: hind foot and fore foot, hind foot and fore foot. The diagonal hind and fore feet are used at the same time. There are many different forms of the trot. The most common are the jog or slow trot that one sits to (most commonly used by the Western rider), the regular or normal trot which is a slightly faster cadence, the extended trot in which the horse goes no faster than the regular trot but extends his forelegs and thus covers more ground, and the fast trot.

The canter is a three-beat gait. Motion again starts with the hind foot, but there is a difference—the horse leads or stretches out one of his forelegs to gain balance. He starts with a hind foot, then uses the diagonal fore and hind feet together, then leads with the other fore foot. If he leads with his right foreleg he is said to be on the right lead. If he leads with his left foreleg, he is on the left lead. There is a fourth motion when all four feet are in the air but, of course, we cannot hear it. A canter or lope, sometimes called the slow gallop, is a very easy gait, really no faster than a regular trot.

The gallop, or fast gallop, is a four-beat gait. The horse begins, for example, in viewing him from his left, with his near (left) hind, then moves to his off (right) hind, then near fore, then off fore. In the full gallop the horse is said to be "flat-out." Horses obviously race at a full gallop.

Canter on the left lead: the horse stretches his left foreleg forward.

Every rider uses aids to maneuver his horse. The style of riding may be different, and it has certainly changed from era to era, but the aids used by the rider have always remained fundamentally the same. The natural aids of the rider are his hands, legs, weight, and voice. The unnatural or artificial aids are crop and spurs.

The rider's hands direct the horse by means of the reins. The English or saddle seat rider steers a horse much as one steers a bicycle. The reins are the handlebars and the horse's head is the wheel in-between. The reins should never be used alone but should be used together with the leg aids. The Western horse and polo pony are neck-reined. These animals are trained to respond and move away from the slightest touch of the reins on the neck. Done correctly, the rider uses his legs and weight in conjunction with reining, although the well-trained animal learns to respond only to the rein.

The knowledgeable rider does not interfere with his horse's head. He allows enough rein for the head to remain in its normal alert position for the work the horse must do. For example, a horse going up a steep hill will extend his neck and head in order to keep his balance while climbing. The reins extend with his head. On a level plane, the horse will bring his head and neck back in naturally because he no longer has to work so hard. The reins should be shortened. A horse uses his neck and his head as his main source of balance, just as we use our arms to help balance us. Hamper the use of his head and neck and the horse can stumble or fall.

The legs are the aids used to make a horse go faster and to control his sideward motion. Because the legs exert pressure to move the hindquarters, and the hindquarters must move first in order for the horse to go, the rider who sits quietly in the saddle and applies strong pressure with his legs will be more successful than the rider who tries to lean forward and push the horse forward with his hands. This is a very common error.

A slow, steady pressure of the legs or many small squeezes will usually get the horse going more quickly than many large belts with the heels. This is because the rider who tries to give a large kick must by necessity remove his leg from the horse's side. Thus, he temporarily loses the advantage of his leg. With practice and training, a horse will learn to respond quickly and easily to one or both of the rider's legs. Smooth action cannot be achieved through force, but only through expertise and finesse.

Correct placement of the rider's weight is an important element in good control. The rider who sits like a lump on his horse will undoubtedly have a horse who responds like one. The horse is sensitive to weight and carries it best at the shoulder. Of course, the rider cannot sit on the horse's shoulder so we compromise and sit in the saddle directly behind it. A horse can handle us quite easily there and he, too, is comfortable. At the same time, if the rider sits too far back or too far forward in the saddle, the horse is not free to perform as he should. He is hampered by the rider's weight. An expert horseman learns to use his weight to his advantage. For example, impulsion (going forward) is achieved by the rider's settling his body weight slightly into his seat bones. Feeling this weight in his hindquarters, the horse responds. He gathers his hindquarters up underneath him and then, when he feels active pressure from the rider's legs, he moves forward. The rider who wishes to stop his horse, squares his shoulders and, again, pushes his weight deep into his seat. The horse feels this drag on his hindquarters and is alert to a new request from the rider. If the rider, while placing his weight back, resists with his reins (he doesn't have to pull, only resist the horse's natural tendency to go forward), the horse will have no recourse but to gather his hindquarters in and stop solidly on all four feet. His head will not fly up in the air and his mouth will not be hurt.

A good Western show rider can do this so superbly from a gallop that it looks as if the horse were going to sit down as he stops. However, the Western rider, as in fact every rider, must be very careful. It is only through experience and much practice that the rider can learn the sensitivity of his horse and know the exact moment when he will respond—at which time pressure of the legs is released and the body moves forward slightly. Most of us do not need to ask our horses to stop so suddenly. Indeed, it would be foolish if we did. A lot less body weight and less

The rider's leg should always be as close behind the withers as possible.

resistance on the reins will bring a horse to a comfortable walk or halt.

A horse's center of balance is directly behind his withers when he is standing. The rider will find his own balance much easier to manage if he learns to use the withers as a guide. If he leans too far forward over the withers he will ultimately lose his balance. Too far back and the same thing will happen. "But," you say, "I've seen people jumping or galloping fast and they are leaning way forward." Take a good look at that rider's legs. They are stationary and firm, as close behind the withers as is physically possible. The rider is only compensating for the speed or rise of his horse by going forward with the upper body. Any good rider, riding any style, will do the same thing when going very fast. A rider can usually keep his balance if he remembers to keep his shoulders in line with his horse's shoulders and his hips in line with his horse's hips.

It is a good idea for all riders to do a few exercises from time to time. Lean forward and touch the horse's ears. Bend down and touch your right foot, your left foot. Start doing the exercises while your horse is standing still. As you become more proficient, increase the gaits until you can do the exercises successfully at all gaits. In doing these exercises you will learn to keep your legs underneath your body where they belong. You will learn not to use your reins to help keep your balance. When I was a small child my instructor had me playing catch in the saddle. I was terrified at first, but I never did fall off as I was sure I would, and I did learn not to rely on my hands to stay aboard.

The voice can also be used to control a horse. For example, a horse who hears the word trot at the same time he is given the aids to trot will learn to trot eventually just by voice command. Remember a horse's hearing is acute. He does not have to be spoken to loudly in order to understand. I discovered the benefit of voice control several years ago, when my son Scott and I were out for a nice, slow ride. I was riding a very large mare, Scott a tiny new pony named Lucky. We had had a lovely ride and were on our way home when (typical of ponies!) Lucky decided we weren't going home fast enough. He scampered away at a fast gallop. Considering the fact that at that time Scott didn't even know how to canter, galloping was pretty frightening. Scott couldn't stop him.

Try if you can to imagine this tiny tiny pony going gallopy gallopy just as fast as his little legs could carry him. My own mare thought this was great sport and was slowly cantering along beside him. My first thought was to grab hold of the pony's reins and try to slow him down. To my dismay I found he was so far below me, I couldn't reach the reins without landing on the ground myself. Then, shades of Roy Rogers and other Western heroes, I tried to grab Scott around the waist and haul him up to me. He was too heavy for me to lift from so far down. What to do? In desperation, I told my son to take his feet out of the stirrups and let go of the reins when I gave the word. This he did. I picked him up by the shirt collar, let the pony go flying out from underneath him, and then deposited him as gently as I could on the ground. Well, that took care of Scott, but I still had a runaway pony to contend with. In sheer frustration I hollered, "Lucky, you stop this minute. Whoa!" Believe it or not, he stopped! After I got over my surprise I began to wonder if it was my voice that had stopped him. I tried again. "Lucky, come here." He came! Perhaps it was coincidence, perhaps he had had some voice training, but since that time, I have never hesitated to use voice control. My friends have mentioned that my voice not only helps control my own horse, but all our horses when they are being ridden alongside of me.

Spurs and crop should be used only by the experienced horseman or in a controlled situation. It takes time to learn to use them correctly. A rider who is not yet experienced does not have full control of his legs or his balance. He may touch his horse with his spurs accidentally at the very time when he shouldn't. Unless you are a *very* experienced rider, roweled spurs are cruel. A blunt-edged spur is the only kind that should be used and then only by a rider who has learned to keep his heels out of the horse's sides. Spurs are used only to accentuate the use of the rider's leg.

A crop should be used on a horse's hindquarters, never on his shoulder or head. There is no better way to frighten or confuse a horse than to hit

Exercises teach you to keep your legs where they belong and help any rider to acquire better balance.

him on the head; and to make matters worse, if you use the crop on the horse's head or shoulder without taking your hand off the reins, you may jerk the reins at a time when it is important for your hands to be quiet. If you need to use a crop, hold the reins in one hand. Apply the crop briskly to the hindquarters with the other hand. One or two quick hard raps are usually enough to inform the horse that you mean business. More is just a waste of time and most often is only a display of the rider's temper. And there is no excuse for that.

I strongly recommend riding lessons. There is no one so expert that he couldn't use a lesson or two. *The major objective of qualified horsemen is to perform every movement with the least amount of effort.* The expert uses his hands, weight, legs, and voice quietly, sometimes all at once, sometimes individually. He makes it look as though the horse were doing the work all by himself. As in every sport, the more ability the person has, the easier it appears to the observer. The horse looks relaxed but alert and gives the impression of vitality held in check but not repressed. The rider appears relaxed, but his back is straight, not stiffly arched inward or slumped outward. His arms are quiet at his side and his legs hardly seem to move at all. A fine rider is always attentive and sensitive to his horse's movements.

A new or inexperienced rider can have a difficult time. Many horses quickly recognize the rider who does not know how to get and maintain control. There are some horses so ornery that they will test every new rider who mounts them. School horses, especially, become wise and are often disobedient. They will try to eat when they should be walking, walk when they should be cantering, or even worse, try to return to the stable against the rider's will. However, perseverance and attention to riding skills will eventually win out, and the rider will feel a flush of victory when he finally succeeds in getting his horse to go where he should when he should. Ponies are notorious for their disobedience. They find that they can often get away with almost anything, since they are usually ridden by small children, and of course most children are not yet well-trained riders.

I repeat. No matter what kind of riding you wish to do, don't ever think you are too good to have a lesson. Especially if you have a horse you cannot control, or one who seems to be developing bad habits despite your work. Most faults of the horse are caused by the errors of the rider.

One of the major faults of riders who have gone beyond the beginning stages of riding is their insistence upon exerting their authority over their horse, *even when it is not necessary.* For lack of a better word, I call this fault "over-riding." In order to turn his horse, the rider uses his strength on the reins to haul him around. In order to make the horse go faster, he kicks hard enough to send a whole field of horses into motion. The rider who knows better than to kick his horse thinks he is riding correctly when he keeps a constant, strong pressure with his legs. As a result, he continually drives his horse forward much faster than he intends. Then he has to use his reins to hold his horse back. The horse is often jerky and bouncy because he can't figure out exactly what his rider wants him to do.

Smooth and gentle use of the aids is the key to success. The less work you and your horse have to do to achieve your aims, the better you both will be. Always start each movement, even on a difficult horse, with the lightest aids possible. Someday they will work, and that is what you have been striving for.

A horse is said to be relaxed but alert when he is flexing. Flexion, in simple terms, is the relaxation of the lower jaw. A horse who is held softly by the reins and accepts his bit with ease is said to be flexing. He often seems to be quietly munching on his bit. The rider will have a finer ride if his horse is flexing, because when a horse is relaxed, his gaits are smoother, he is much more receptive to the rider's wishes and he will respond quickly and easily.

If you see a horse's head suddenly fly up in the air, or his mouth open wide, you know the rider is putting too much pressure on the reins and has poor rein control. If you see a horse who won't stand still or who goes much too fast unnecessarily, look for too much leg. If you see a horse whose hindquarters appear to be dragging, look for the rider who is placing his

Flexion. When a horse is flexing, he is relaxed, but alert, his gaits are smoother, and he will respond quickly and easily.

weight too far back in the saddle. This could be very dangerous while going over fences.

Young horses or green, untrained horses will do many of these things and much more. They are like athletes who may be strong but who don't yet know how to use and control their bodies. The trainer has to work a long time to make the horse understand what is expected of him. Often, the trainer not only has to work with the natural faults of the horse, but with the faults the horse has acquired to protect himself from the ignorance of his past rider.

Many riders like to have a horse with spirit. They enjoy the battle that goes with a horse who bucks, rears, and bounces around continuously. Every horse who feels good will do a certain amount of this, but if it continues day in and day out, that rider has achieved nothing with his horse. To me, that particular horse is disobedient and/or spoiled. It is proof that he has an unknowledgeable rider and no horseman on his back. Once a horse is sufficiently trained, there is no excuse for disobedience. There is no such thing as a "too fit" horse. He is either too well fed for the amount of exercise he is given or he is misbehaving.

Watch your horse. Watch the horses around you. Read some books. Go to horse shows. Find out the best that can be achieved by you and your horse within your own limitations. Be proud of your riding skills and learn, learn, learn. Be a horseman not a rider.

When riding, check the girth or cinch from time to time and tighten if necessary.

11

Care of Your Horse
While Riding

Riding horses is dangerous. Never forget that for a minute. Everyone, no matter how good he is, is going to take a spill sooner or later. Those are the odds. But there is no reason to go out looking for a spill. First, find yourself a horse *you* can ride. If you can't ride him, have him trained or sell him. Don't play games with your life.

When saddling up, don't plunk your saddle down hard on your horse's back. His skin is thin in that area and his back is very sensitive. Set the saddle on gently at the withers and slide it back slightly in the direction of the horse's hair. If you use a saddle pad, see that it is not wrinkled under the saddle. When a saddle is first fastened, never pull the girth as tightly as you can. Tightening a girth suddenly can make a horse constrict and suffer real pain. He may even fall as a result. Many horses have learned to protect themselves by puffing out their bellies. Put the saddle on gently and walk the horse a few paces. He will soon relax and then you can adjust the girth.

Check the bridle to be sure it fits firmly but not tightly, and to see that no part of your equipment is twisted. Often in cleaning, the pieces of the bridle are not put back together properly. Don't forget to clean out the

Posting is the up-down motion the English and saddle seat rider use while trotting.

horse's feet with a hoof pick. Too much junk in his feet can make for slippery footing, especially when crossing roads or other smooth surfaces, and a stone lodged in his foot for any length of time could cause a bruise. After mounting, check the girth for slack and see that the stirrups are set comfortably. Double-check the girth later on if you are out on a long ride. You may find it necessary to shorten the slack again.

"Walk the first mile" is an old adage that should not be ignored. Walking the first mile gives your horse time to limber up and gives you time to get situated in the saddle. All athletes do exercises to limber up before they perform. Animals need that time, too.

Don't make a habit of galloping continuously. Alternating the gaits produces a well-muscled and well-conditioned horse. The change in gaits has an added advantage—it keeps your horse from getting bored. The rider who travels the same route every day should concentrate on varying his routine. The horse will be far more responsive because he must pay attention to his rider to learn what he is going to do next. Horses won't forget. Trot or canter in the same place every time and they will soon strike off in that gait whether it is asked for or not. Very undesirable.

Hard surfaces, like roads, are extremely dangerous. They are not only slippery, but if your horse pounds on them for any length of time, his legs and feet will suffer. Sidebone, arthritis, and other bone and leg problems can occur. Hard frozen ground is included in this category, too. Always walk on hard surfaces.

While on the subject of ground—soft, boggy places are equally dangerous. The least that could happen while going fast through a bog is that your horse could lose a shoe. The worst is a pulled muscle or even a broken leg. Slow down through these areas and try to pick out the best footing.

Too many people ignore these simple and obvious rules. They gallop through everything, and over everything, and then wonder why their horse eventually ends up lame. Then they have to buy a new horse because the old one just won't go anymore. This is not to say that one shouldn't go out on a fast ride if he wishes. Just ride your horse with his well-being in mind. And make sure he is in tip-top condition before you go galloping many miles cross-country.

Good conditioning will help any horse. There is nothing better for his muscles and endurance than working up slowly to many long, even trots up and down hills. Fox hunters thrive on this sort of training. It does wonders for some of the weight problems you might have, too.

Ring work is especially good to keep your horse in correct balance for the movement you want him to execute. If you are not fortunate enough to have a ring available, try using obstacles on the trail. Keep your horse trotting in a straight line when you find a flat stretch of land. Most untrained horses tend to wander. Does yours? Try, when approaching a tree at a turn, to make the horse use his whole body by using your inside leg pressed firmly at his side to bend or curve him around that tree. Besides making your horse more supple and more responsive to your legs, you will rid him of the horrible habit of shaving trees as he goes around them. Most horses will allow room for themselves on a narrow trail but they don't often take into consideration that there is a rider involved. I don't know a rider who hasn't had his knees cracked at one time or another.

Posting is the forward rising motion the English and saddle seat rider use while trotting. Posting allows the rider to maintain his seat more comfortably in the saddle. The rising motion also relieves the horse of the rider's weight—for short moments the rider gives his horse's hind legs a rest.

While trail riding the rider who posts should determine which of his horse's forelegs is touching the ground when he sits down in the saddle. If he sits for the first trot when the horse's right foreleg touches the ground, he should remember to reverse the procedure the next time he trots and sit when the left foreleg touches the ground. Many horses until they are well trained prefer one side to the other. A sensitive rider will notice that each time he starts to trot, the horse will force him to be in the saddle when the favored or stronger leg hits the ground. On very long trail rides, some professionals advise the rider to accept the favored leg more often while trotting. Since it is the stronger leg, the horse will carry his rider more comfortably for a longer time.

The untrained horse usually prefers to lead with one particular leg when he canters, too. If the horse is allowed to continue doing this at both the trot and the canter he can become one-sided: well muscled and supple on one side, underdeveloped and stiff on the other. The rider can help his horse by deliberately alternating his leads each time there is a canter. Teach a horse to go willingly and comfortably on either lead. Otherwise, if he is turning in one direction but is trying to lead with the opposite leg, he may become confused. The rider just may find himself on the ground because his horse got his feet tangled.

Keep well to the side of the road if you must ride on one. Even dirt roads are dangerous today. It is not uncommon for drivers to come zooming up on you and your horse, honk the horn, and wave. By that time your horse may have the heebie-jeebies, and you'll be sure you are going to be tossed any minute. Unfortunately there are even some drivers who will sideswipe an animal on the road. To this day, Sam is frightened of paved roads in rainy weather. He was sideswiped on a very rainy day when he was three years old and he has never forgotten. I think some drivers like to see the horses bounce around. It looks exciting and they don't realize the danger in which they are placing the riders. Of course, there are other people who are just plain malicious. So be careful. Remember also that a horse is just as likely to swerve into danger when frightened as he is to run away from it. If a car is coming toward you at high speed and your horse seems frightened, put up your hand to show the driver that you want him to slow down. If you are not on a major highway, and you don't belong on a major highway until you are absolutely sure of the behavior of your horse, the driver will probably obey your request.

It is not uncommon to meet noisy motorcycles or snowmobiles on trails that used to be exclusively for horses. Do your best to slow them down, too. If you have the chance, explain to the drivers why you are asking them

Horses often "spook" at unfamiliar things. Today a buggy is pretty unfamiliar.

to slow down. Next time you meet them it might turn out to be a more pleasant experience.

A rider who runs away from dangers that his horse is likely to meet often, teaches his horse that running away is the correct thing to do. Wouldn't you look silly if one day you and a friend were out peacefully riding and chatting and you neglected to notice that a motorcycle was approaching. The next minute there you are in the far field struggling with your horse while your friend stands there with his mouth open.

Horses can be timid creatures. Our hunt often meets in Amish country. As a result, many horses are meeting noisy horse buggies for the first time and are scared to death of them. At the same time the Amish horses are meeting big, terrifying-looking horse vans for the first time and are scared to death of them. The unfamiliar can be frightening. But they all learn.

If you ride in a group, lead sometimes, follow other times. Teach your horse confidence both in himself and his rider. No matter where he happens to be. If he's unhappy leaving other horses, practice leaving them often. If he persists in giving you a bouncy ride because he's not first in line, be patient with his theatrics, but insist he follow. If he's frightened of some obstacle and balks, don't be ashamed to take a lead from an older and wiser horse. Your horse can learn confidence from him, too. Pay attention to your horse. Your riding will take on new dimensions.

After you have had your fun, walk the last mile home. Your horse will not only be relaxed but will be "cooled out." If he's worked up a sweat, it will dry and make a lot less work for you or his groom. When you get home, remove the saddle and bridle and rub off the saddle and bridle marks. Feel your horse's chest with your hand. If he still feels hot, walk him until he is cool. You'll be able to tell the difference. If you have made the effort to walk that last mile home, you will need to walk him only a few minutes, if at all. Never turn a hot horse loose in a stall. There is no better way to ask him to get sick.

12

Manners While Riding

Every rider should have good manners. They are not just for show—they protect you and your horse.

Pay attention to the land over which you are riding. Most of us are not fortunate enough to own all the land we ride on. We are riding on land through the courtesy of the landowner. Respect his wishes. Don't ride on the nice green lawn he has worked so hard on. The holes a horse can make are disastrous. Don't ride close by his house unless you know ahead of time that you are welcome. You are infringing upon his privacy. Don't go exploring barns or other horse pastures unless you have been invited. It is rude, annoying, and truly none of your business. Every gate you pass through should be left the way you found it. If it was closed, leave it that way. Should you happen to knock down a fence (God forbid!) or damage other property, either repair it or inform the owner and offer to make restitution.

A farmer will not take lightly a horse galloping or even walking over his plowed fields. He's worked hard to cultivate them. Stay away or skirt them. If you're not the farmer type, be even more careful. Many fields appear to be uncultivated to the uneducated eye.

Riders who ignore these simple rules are bound to meet a fence barring their way the next time they wish to go through. It is not unheard of to meet a shotgun either. Unfortunately the careless rider has not only ruined his own sport, he's spoiled the riding trails for others, too.

If the weather is very wet, don't canter through the fields. All you'll do is grind up the soil and make nice big holes. Chop it up enough and the ground will dry unevenly and spoil the footing for you and for others on the dry days. A major gripe of mine.

If you are riding alone and meet a group, don't gallop up to them. Slow your horse down and approach them quietly. Do the same when leaving a group. The riders left behind will appreciate your thoughtfulness. Many horses will catch the excitement of a new arrival or a misbehaving horse and react accordingly. Similarly, don't walk away from a friend who is trying to mount. He'll have a terrible time keeping his horse still, as his horse will want to catch up with yours.

When riding in a group, keep your distance. A horse's length apart is the general rule, but if you can't figure that out, stay back far enough so that you can see the heels of the horse in front of you. This applies if you ride on a trail or in a ring.

No one likes a kicker. If you have one, tie a red ribbon in his tail to warn others that your horse flies out. Many horses aren't true kickers, but they will kick if they find their heels stepped on by a crowding horse. In that case the horse is only defending himself as far as I'm concerned, but if he finds his mark, the result can be just as damaging, so kicking should be prevented if possible.

If you are jumping in a group, keep even more distance. As the saying goes, "Give your friend room to fall in." It would be a frightful shock to find yourself in the air looking down on the body of your friend lying right where your horse's feet are about to land. If your horse continually refuses jumps, take yourself to the back of the group. It is inconsiderate to hold everyone back because your horse is disobedient.

If you are leading a group on the trail, go no faster than the poorest

A jump with poor footing on the approach, probably because riders use the jump when the ground is muddy.

rider can safely manage. There is a crack-the-whip effect when trail riding. The horse in front may be trotting but the horse in the rear will have to gallop to keep up. Give the horse in the rear time to catch his breath, to say nothing of the rider.

Don't try to hold low branches for the rider behind you. It's a nice thought, but if you do, you will most likely hold them just long enough to swing them right back into his face. Bend down and go through brush as quietly as you can.

There is a group of hand signals that make life easier for the trail rider. The fist up twice means trot. The fist up three times means canter. The hand straight up means slow down or stop. A finger pointed toward the ground indicates some sort of danger (i.e., a hole or the like). What a pleasure it is to ride behind someone who is willing to let you know what is happening before it happens.

The rider who shares an indoor arena or a ring with others should always enter quietly so as not to interfere with the horses and riders already working. If the ring is crowded, all the horses should go in the same direction, remembering to reverse from time to time. If you prefer to go at a faster gait than the others, pass on the outside if it is at all convenient. If it isn't, announce quietly that you will be passing right or left as the case may be.

The disobedient and unruly horse should leave the ring unless given permission to stay. That horse may upset every other horse in the ring. Wait until there are fewer people and, therefore, less danger of an accident.

If you are using the ring while others are taking a lesson, be quiet. That is not the time for loud discussions with your friends.

If someone falls off, stop your horse immediately. A loose horse will usually trot up to another horse and stand quietly as long as everyone is still.

Actually, manners are nothing but good common sense and consideration. Please remember them.

13

Your Horse's Health

The practice of veterinary medicine requires a great deal of knowledge and skill. Today a veterinarian must complete six or more years of hard study before he qualifies for his degree. Don't ever hesitate to call a vet when in doubt. He's been well trained to care for your horses.

Everyone who owns horses should have a good book on veterinary medicine. As each book will tell you, books should not be used in place of a vet but should be used to help you recognize illness and prevent problems. Vets, like other doctors, seem to have a vocabulary all their own, so to help you understand what you are reading here are a few of the most common words and their meanings.

Ball: A pill.

Drench: A liquid medicine given orally with a syringe.

Electuary: Drugs gooped up with honey or syrup and smeared on the tongue and back teeth. The horse eventually swallows it. Administered when the throat is so swollen and sore that neither a ball nor a drench can be given.

Poultice: A soft composition, usually heated and spread on a cloth, applied to a sore or inflamed part of the body, usually the foot.

Liniment: A liquid that produces a small irritation. Applied by massage which helps to increase blood circulation.

Blister: An even stronger irritant which causes an accumulation of fluids between layers of skin. The top layer falls off and a new layer of skin forms.

Firing: The strongest irritant, used for the treatment of bone trouble. A hot iron with sharp points that hardly pierce the skin is applied. This causes a local inflammation which brings an increased blood supply to the area and thus promotes the growth of tissue to strengthen the area as it heals.

GENERAL HEALTH CARE

There are a number of things you should do to keep your horse healthy and happy. Please keep his well-being in mind. And remember, it's often much easier to prevent a problem than it is to cure it.

Fatigue: You know how you feel when you've had some pretty strong exercise. A good, hot bath, maybe some liniment, and rest are your cures. A horse isn't any different except that a bath isn't advisable in anything but warm weather. However, liniment rubbed on sore muscles will feel good to your horse and so will bandages on his legs. Bandages here serve the same purpose for horses that support hosiery does for people. A nice clean stall with plenty of bedding will help him rest. Perhaps a small bran mash as a laxative or even a shot of whiskey can be given if the going has been exceptionally long and difficult. Hold off water and other feed until he's had a chance to get himself back together again.

Grooming: Horses need to be groomed. Obviously every horse will look better with a well-brushed coat and a neat mane and tail. Furthermore, removing caked dirt and mud from under a saddle and bridle will help to prevent sores. Grooming also stimulates circulation and thus makes for a healthier and happier horse.

Always curry in a circular motion, in the direction the hair is growing. Do not use a curry comb below the knee. Your horse has very thin legs from the knee down and currying could damage sensitive tendons.

He will appreciate a good, brisk brushing. Use the brush slowly but firmly around his head. Sponge out his eyes and nostrils gently with clean warm water. When combing or brushing his mane and tail, separate a few hairs at a time. Son can't stand having his mane combed. Obviously it hurts. We do our best to be as gentle as possible and—there is no better word for it—we persevere!

A pastured horse is better left with a longer mane and tail than the manes and tails one sees in the show ring. Flies and other bugs are a problem in the pasture, and the poor horse should have every means of protection possible. However, there is no harm in thinning out an overly thick mane so that it can lie flat and thus look neater. This is done by pulling out a small bit of hair at a time. Always pull out the long hairs from the underside of the mane. I find that wrapping a few hairs at a time around a small comb and then pulling is the easiest method.

Don't forget to clean out the feet. Feet must be cleaned to assure proper growth and vitality of shoe and frog. The foot needs to breathe. Any stones, pebbles, or other sharp fragments which have become lodged in the hoof must be removed, too.

Bathing: Watch out when washing a horse. Make sure the weather is good and warm. A horse is more susceptible to colds than you are. Usually, if you don't mind getting wet while you are bathing your horse, the weather is warm enough for him. Walk him until he dries. It won't take long.

Whether you use a bona fide horse shampoo or one of your own, be careful. The first time my husband and daughter washed our horses they were very generous with the shampoo. The result was suds everywhere, and we ended up with the cleanest barn in town.

Mare in season, in heat: Most mares come in season about every three weeks, from February to July, and remain in heat for three or four days.

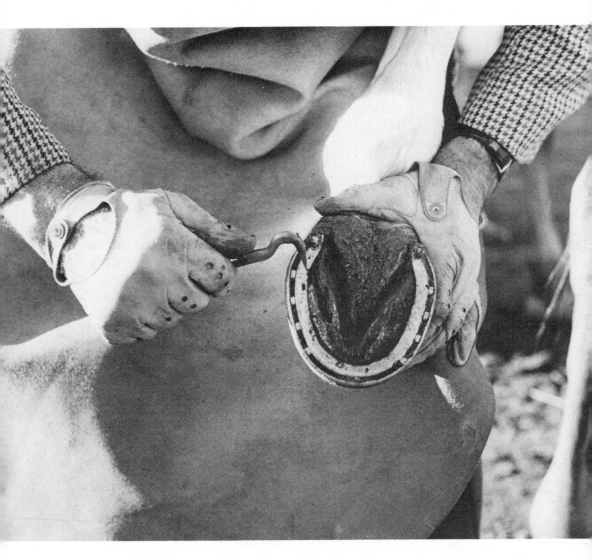

Cleaning the hoof with a hoof pick. Work with the pick going away from you and remove all foreign matter.

When a mare is in heat she may be erratic. She may fuss for no reason, she may be unwilling to do her work. She may even bite or kick. Some mares are quieter than others during this period so watch for signs in your own mare. Be very careful around her if she happens to be one of the more nervous types.

Scratches and cuts: Horses who live out in pasture or travel on trails are constantly getting themselves skinned and scratched. Unless they are very deep and/or jagged, you can care for these cuts yourself. Wash them thoroughly and apply antiseptic just as you would to a cut or scrape of your own.

If the wound was caused by wire or some other unsanitary item, or is exceptionally deep, call the vet for a tetanus and antibiotic shot. Watch carefully for infection but don't be in a hurry for the wound to heal. A clean wound is bound to heal eventually, and the important thing is that it heal from the inside out. When it has healed, apply Vaseline to promote the regrowth of hair.

Saddle and bridle sores: Saddle and bridle sores are most often caused by ill-fitting and dirty saddles and bridles. Girth sores are the most common. Proper attention to cleanliness and correct adjustment will virtually eliminate the problem. A horse who hasn't been ridden in a long while will have a soft back and belly. Don't ride him long or hard at first, but wait until he has had time to toughen. Pinched skin under the girth is bound to develop a sore. If one does occur, wash and apply antiseptic just as you would for scratches and cuts. If you can arrange it, don't ride your horse until the sore is well healed.

Saddle sores are unpleasant. Too much hard riding before your horse has been conditioned, an ill-fitting saddle, a saddle that has been allowed to become hard and brittle through lack of care, and dirt under the saddle are all causes of saddle sores. Sores can be difficult to cure so don't work your horse until they have healed.

Curb sores are the result of a curb chain or strap that is either too tight or twisted.

All of these sores occur because of the rider's negligence. Always check equipment and be aware of your horse's general physical condition.

Tooth care: A horse's teeth are generally very healthy. He doesn't seem to have the problem with cavities that we do. Sometimes irregular growth of the edges of the cheek teeth does occur and then they need to be repaired. The upper molars may become sharp on their outer edges and injure the inside of the cheeks. The lower molars may get sharp on the inner edges hurting the tongue. Either way a horse has trouble eating. Sometimes a horse who fusses with the bit in his mouth is showing a symptom of tooth trouble. The process of removing those sharp edges is called *floating*. Your vet should handle this.

Foot care, shoeing: Successful hoof growth depends upon good care. A healthy horse with good clean food, lots of exercise, and enough moisture will have a healthy, shiny foot. The hoof never seems to grow evenly so it needs to be trimmed to prevent jagged edges which could eventually tear and cause pain. A hoof that is too long keeps a horse from standing straight on the ground and eventually causes lameness.

A horse's hoof is divided into four parts: the wall, the bar, the sole, and the frog. The wall is the outer shell that goes from the hair to the ground. The bar is the part extending from the wall inward toward the point of the frog. The bar carries the weight of the horse and helps protect the frog. The frog is the V-shaped mass that is in between the bars. It is important, as it cushions shock, aids in preventing slipping, and acts as a pump which sends the blood from the foot back up the leg. For these reasons, the frog should *never* be cut.

The shoe is an artificial base of support. A horse needs shoes to protect his feet and to keep them from wearing out too fast. Good trimming and shoeing can compensate for minor defects in a horse's legs and feet.

In the past, horses were the major means of transportation. Every town had at least one farrier (a blacksmith who specializes in shoeing horses) to care for the horses' feet. As cars and other means of transportation came into prominence, the trade dwindled. As a result, finding a good black-

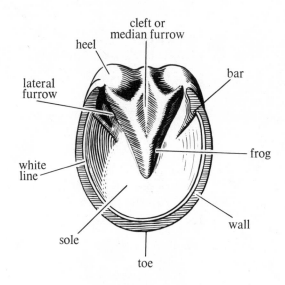

cleft or
median furrow

heel

bar

lateral
furrow

frog

white
line

wall

sole

toe

PARTS OF THE FOOT

smith today is difficult. Getting him to come when you need him is even more difficult. Finally, as a result of this shortage of blacksmiths, classes in shoeing are sprouting up throughout the country. But don't relax. The classes haven't graduated enough farriers yet.

Be selective in your choice of blacksmith. Many leg problems are caused by improper shoeing and/or neglect of the feet. A farrier must have solid knowledge of the physiology of a horse's feet and legs. He must know how a horse should stand and how he should move. Look for the man who has the respect and approval of other horsemen in the area. Investigate his experience and talk with him about horses. Be aware of his manner around them. A quiet person, naturally, will be more desirable. If he owns his own horses, chances are he will be even more knowledgeable. Find out if he is willing to use a forge or if he will only cold shoe. Every foot is different. The shoe should be hot and shaped to the horse's natural foot, not the other way around. Find out if he is reliable. It won't really matter how talented a man he is if he can't come when he is needed.

A good blacksmith will notice any defects in your horse's legs and feet and try to correct them. Sam has a tendency to toe in slightly. It hasn't been too serious, but as a youngster he did a lot of stumbling which could have been dangerous. Thanks to our blacksmith, Sam now walks straight while shod and is surefooted even in his bare feet.

A horse's shoes are selected on the basis of the kind of work he is expected to do. There are many different kinds so be sure to tell the blacksmith how you plan to use your horse. A horse doing a lot of road work will need a shoe that is very different from the shoe of a horse going cross-country.

Plan on having your horses shod every four to eight weeks. This time varies depending on your horse, the time of year, and the work he is doing.

If there is a season in your part of the country when you don't wish to ride, feel free to pull the shoes and let the horse go barefoot. It's good for him. Do remember to keep his hooves trimmed, however, to avoid tearing. And do keep his feet clean.

COMMON ILLNESSES

Horses get sick and feel pain just as deeply as we do. We must watch constantly for signs of their discomfort because for the most part they suffer in silence.

A horse's heart averages 36 to 40 beats per minute. The pulse can be felt under either side of the jaw where there is a large artery. Find the artery, then count the beats for 15 seconds, then multiply by four. Another good place for pulse-taking is the artery on the inside of the foreleg near the elbow. The normal temperature for a horse is 99 to 101 degrees. It is always taken rectally with a regular horse or large-animal thermometer.

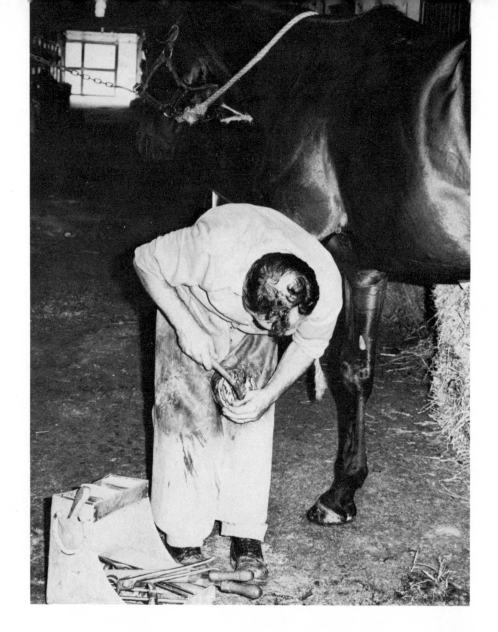

Be selective in your choice of blacksmith.

Colic: Colic is a common illness in horses. The simplest description is that the horse has a stomachache. Unfortunately, a horse does not have the ability to vomit. The only way he can get rid of his pain, and it is severe, is through the bowels. Some of the causes of colic are: overfeeding, poor watering, eating rich foods (like grass or apples) when not accustomed to it. A twisted gut is a form of colic which is caused by a stumble, a fall, or too heavy a feed given after a long day's work. The symptoms of colic are pronounced. The horse may sweat. He bites at and sometimes kicks at his side. He may repeatedly lie down and get up again. He may roll while on the ground.

If your horse is down, encourage him to get up and walk. Cover him with a blanket to keep him warm. After walking awhile (sometimes a couple of hours) his bowels should be stimulated and gas should be eliminated. If he still shows signs of discomfort, continue walking. A horse in extreme discomfort or one who is down and cannot be forced up is one very sick horse. Call the vet fast. Your horse can die. If you have a colic remedy at hand, give it to him. An enema may help too, but I'd rather the vet took care of that.

Azoturia (Monday Morning Sickness): No one honestly knows why this sickness occurs. It is believed that it occurs in a well-conditioned, well-fed horse when his daily ration of feed is not reduced when his activity is substantially decreased. There is stiffness in the hindquarters and he may drag his hind legs. He has difficulty urinating. Perspiration is evident and he may quiver. He may fall and not be able to rise. Keep the horse quiet and covered and call the vet immediately. Cutting down on a horse's feed when he is not working seems usually to prevent the problem.

Cold: A horse catches a cold similar to that caught by humans. He can catch it either from standing in drafts or from infection. A cold need not be serious if it is discovered early and the horse is rested in a warm, well-ventilated stall. He may sneeze, his nose will run, his eyes will water. He may or may not have a fever. He may or may not have a cough. Colds are dangerous if not cared for so don't ignore them. Call the vet if he can't shake it.

Flu: Flu flies around horses just as it does around humans. If one of your horses catches it, you can rest assured the others will probably catch it too. The horse will go off his feed, show signs of fever and cough, and have a nasal discharge. Antibiotics are needed. Remember, horses should have yearly flu shots.

Heaves: Another name for the heaves is *broken wind.* The lungs deteriorate and the horse seems to heave as he breathes. When he is exercised, he becomes short of breath. A horse with heaves will never be of much use. Although I've talked to many horsemen who feel they can cure this ailment, I have never seen them succeed. Sometimes allergies are confused with heaves because the symptoms appear to be the same, but allergies can be treated successfully. Only an X-ray can differentiate between the two. Good ventilation, non-dusty stalls and hay, and proper attention to correct feeding will help prevent heaves or allergies. Also, be sure not to work a horse hard unless he is in condition.

There are diseases and viruses that are prevalent in each area of the country. It is always wise to check with your veterinarian to see if there are preventive shots available. As with humans, new viruses and diseases crop up from time to time. Keep your ears and eyes open. Never hesitate to question your vet if you hear of or read about something new that may travel into your area. Check with your vet, too, if you plan to ship your horse to another area. His advice could save your horse.

PARASITES

Horses are susceptible to parasites. Almost all horses have worms to some degree but they are not harmful when kept under control. If your horse has been eating well but doesn't seem to put on weight and his coat remains sallow, you should suspect worms. The most common worms are stomach bots, intestinal or round worms, red large and small strongyles, and pin worms.

Stomach bots: These are not really worms but come from a yellowish-brown fly (the bot fly) who lays its eggs on the horse's legs. They look like little yellow dots. Some authorities say the horse licks his legs and the eggs are transferred to the stomach where they hatch and become stomach bots. Others claim the worm hatches and burrows into the skin. Either way they end up in the stomach. Bots are about three-quarters of an inch long and may be expelled with the droppings. If you see any of these yellow eggs on your horse, scrape them off or wash them off with warm water as soon as possible and destroy them.

Intestinal worms: These worms are probably the commonest in young horses and I believe look the ugliest. When they are found they are white, stiff, and up to a foot in length. They can be as thick as a pencil. In large numbers they cause stoppage or irregularity of the bowels and even colic. Loss of condition becomes obvious.

Large and small strongyles: These worms, or blood worms as they are sometimes called, are the most dangerous because they pass through the bowel wall into the blood vessels. They can cause symptoms of colic and even a blood clot. They are reddish in color and up to half an inch long. The bowels are irregular and diarrhea is present. The worms are difficult to see without a microscope.

Pin worms: Pin worms live in the rectum. They are about one and three-quarter inches long and very thin. The horse rubs his tail and there is a sticky discharge at the anus.

You should get a veterinarian's advice about all worms. There are many different varieties of worm medicine on the market. Usually they are administered every six to eight weeks and are given with the daily ration of food.

I prefer to have the vet come twice a year with a particularly strong liquid dosage of worm medicine appropriate to the time of year and the type of worms prevalent at that time. A tube is sent up the horse's nostril, down through the esophogus, and directly into his stomach. It isn't very pretty to see, but the procedure is not painful, and it does get rid of most of the worms. Don't be surprised if your horse feels poorly the next day.

Many stable owners keep their horses in their stalls or in a small paddock in order to confine the worms as they are eliminated. Then they put their horses elsewhere and clean and disinfect the soiled area. There is less danger of the horses' recontaminating themselves this way. Worms die immediately when reaching the air, but the eggs continue to live. They rest on the grass or hay, the horses eat them, and thus the cycle starts all over again.

LEG AND FOOT PROBLEMS

A sound horse is a horse who can walk, trot, and canter freely on all four legs. A horse has very poor circulation in his lower legs. Therefore, his legs will often be the first thing to be affected if his owner has been negligent. Lameness can be the result of overwork and overfeeding as well as some of the more obvious causes.

Founder or laminitis: In simple terms founder is an inflammation of a sensitive part which connects the hoof to the fleshy part of the foot. It can be painful. Founder is caused by overfeeding, eating improper foods, exhaustion and overwork, long work over hard roads, or even drinking cold water when hot and sweating.

If your horse makes an uncalled for trip to the feed bin and consumes a large amount of oats, watch for founder. Riders who take their horses out for long, difficult rides when the horse is not in condition can expect founder. Properly treated, founder can be cured. If left to its own devices, founder becomes increasingly serious. Call the vet for advice.

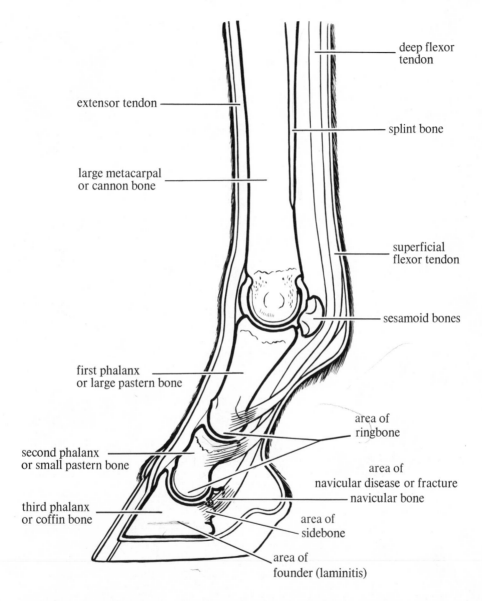

extensor tendon

deep flexor tendon

large metacarpal or cannon bone

splint bone

superficial flexor tendon

sesamoid bones

first phalanx or large pastern bone

area of ringbone

second phalanx or small pastern bone

area of navicular disease or fracture

navicular bone

third phalanx or coffin bone

area of sidebone

area of founder (laminitis)

PARTS OF THE FOOT AND LOCATIONS OF SOME LEG AND FOOT PROBLEMS

Splint: Often one hears the saying "he popped a splint." The splint is a bony enlargement on the cannon bone or splint bones usually on the inside of the front legs. Sometimes one can barely see a splint and only by running the hand down a horse's leg can it be discovered.

Splints can be caused by overexertion or lots of hard work on hard surfaces. They are fairly common among young horses who play hard in the pasture.

Racehorses often have splints. Call the vet for advice because treatment can vary.

Sprains and strains: These are pretty obvious and usually you know how your horse managed to get them. Sometimes a horse out on rough pasture will catch his foot in a hole or slip on some ice. If your horse doesn't seem to be in too much pain, rest will take care of the problem. Liniment rubbed on the inflamed area will feel good. If lameness persists, or your horse seems to be feeling worse, better call the vet. There is a time for hot treatment and a time for cold treatment.

Sidebone, ringbone, and navicular disease: All three may cause severe lameness and in the case of navicular disease, there is no absolute cure. Sidebone is a bony enlargement on the sides just above the hoof. Ringbone is a bony enlargement that goes all the way around the leg just above the hoof. Sometimes the bone ossifies; the horse registers no pain at all, and he appears sound in every way. Other times a horse is in great pain and vet bills climb and climb. We have had horses with both reactions. Our quarter horse appears to have sidebone but has never taken a lame step —from sidebone, that is. Another horse we needed to X-ray simply to discover that she had sidebone, but she was in extreme pain and could not be ridden. If the sidebone or ringbone is not painful there is nothing to worry about unless you plan to work your horse heavily over a long period of time or you wish to show him. In some classes points are taken off for flaws in conformation.

Navicular disease is always serious. In simple language, it is an ulcer on the navicular bone in the foot. Usually it is caused by hard work on hard roads, although bad shoeing can also cause it. Sometimes navicular disease can be spotted because the horse will point his toes when he walks. There is a lot of research going on to devise a cure for this disease but at this time the treatment is only partially successful. Most often the owner is forced to put the horse down.

Mud fever: Mud fever can be compared to chapped hands in human beings. It affects the lower part of the leg and foot and is caused by muddy, wet, cold weather. Many riders feel they are doing their horse a favor by washing his legs after a muddy ride. This is not true. Instead, bandage the legs loosely for an hour or so to keep them warm while the mud dries. Then remove the bandages and brush off the mud. When horses are turned out to pasture in cold, muddy weather, let the feathers on the back of the ankles and fetlocks grow long. This is a good way to protect your horse, since the feathers gather the mud and moisture and the skin is not bothered. From time to time brush the dried mud from his legs. It will help stimulate circulation and will help prevent infection.

Don't bandage a horse so tightly that circulation is stopped. Put the padding on smoothly so that there are no wrinkles, then start the bandage in the middle of the lower leg. Wind down around the fetlock and then work your way back up to finish just below the knee. I repeat. Circulation is very poor in a horse's lower leg. Be careful.

Thrush: Thrush is an infection of the frog in the horse's foot. Thrush smells terrible and a discharge can be seen coming from the center and sides of the frog. In some cases the horse may lose the outer shell of the frog. If the horse is well cared for another shell will form. If the disease is allowed to fester and go deeper, the problem becomes much more serious because the main part of the frog will not replace itself.

There are many thrush medicines, since this is a very common disease. The foot must be well cleaned and medicine should be applied as prescribed. A veterinarian or farrier can advise you. The treatment varies depending upon the seriousness of the infection.

Supposedly the most common causes of thrush are filthy stables or standing a horse in water and mud for long periods of time without cleaning or drying his feet. However, I have seen thrush occur in some stables that are completely dry and immaculate. This leads me to believe that a horse's foot thrives best when it gets a good dose of both wet and dry. Naturally, filthy stalls can lead to contamination, but good, clean mud will not do much harm if your horse's feet are cleaned regularly. Thrush is contagious. Better not to have it at all.

There are many, many more leg problems. I have mentioned only those that are the most common. They occur mainly because of the owner's ignorance and sloth. Horses have their own sensitive areas just as people have theirs. Some tend toward more stomach upsets than others. Some have weaker bones than others. Sooner or later any horse-owner is bound to come across a problem. How foolish he is to ask for those he could possibly avoid through care and better management. Let me remind you also to respect the age and maturation process of your own horse. It is a tragic fact that many horses are broken down and unsound before they are eight years old. Their owners gave no thought to their capabilities.

14

Horses and Children

Horses are wonderful creatures. They can teach a child responsibility, patience, courage, and humility. Owning a horse is a thrill and a delight, and yes, a frustration.

A child sees his riding ability through his own eyes, not through the eyes of an experienced horseman. To the child his riding accomplishments appear exciting and marvelous. It's a long way up to the top of a horse and the jouncing and bouncing a beginner and novice put up with is difficult indeed. As soon as the child begins to feel relatively secure in the saddle he considers himself a good rider. Of course he should feel accomplishment. But riding is an art, an infinitely subtle art. It takes many years of trial, error, and hard work to become a horseman. Learning to stay aboard is only the beginning.

To parents who know little of riding, a child's success is a great achievement. No parent can help but be prejudiced in favor of his child. Parents should keep this in mind when their child comes to them with stars in his eyes and says, "All I want is a horse of my own. I PROMISE I'll take care of him. You won't have to do a thing. And anyway, I know how to ride. I went to Camp Blankety-Blank for two years and we did lots of riding."

Wow! That sales pitch is difficult to resist. What is even worse, many parents believe every word their child is saying.

If you are a parent, and after reading this book you still want to give your child a horse (and I hope you will), take some precautionary measures for safety's sake. Analyze your child's riding ability with open eyes. If you can't, find someone who can. When it comes to finding the right horse for him, your caution will prove invaluable.

Accept before you start that the conscientious parent will be involved with his child's horse; especially if the horse is to live at home. The child will get sick or be invited to a friend's house and suddenly the responsibility of caring for and feeding the horse will fall upon the parent's shoulders. Now, feeding the fish in a bowl in the house is one thing; tramping to the barn on a cold, rainy day is quite another. Chances are that when feeding time comes, father is tired and mother is equally so. Rest assured, there are times when even the most accomplished of horsemen don't feel like tending their horses. But they know, and you must understand, that it must be done.

Mucking out stalls is a chore. Children tire of it quickly. Their idea of owning a horse is to ride it, not to attend to all the necessary incidentals. Children are children. They get angry—at themselves, at parents, and at their horses. One afternoon I arrived at a friend's stable to find him furious. His story was not unusual. The barn needed mucking out. This chore was his child's responsibility. However, his child had been invited to a last-minute party and, of course, wanted to go. After much loud discussion between parent and child, they agreed that since the horses were dependent upon them for every comfort, the child could go to the party but he would have to clean the stalls first and, therefore, arrive a bit late. "A sensible solution," thought my friend. Well, the child did clean out the stalls, but he was so angry about being late to his party that he dumped the entire load of manure right in the center of the barn entrance. Unfortunately, teaching a child responsibility is sometimes tedious and always difficult. Be prepared.

All children are forgetful. They forget to close gates and the horses quickly disappear down the road. Children forget to close stall doors and the horses get out and help themselves to enough oats to feed six horses for ten weeks. If you manage to escape without the horses' getting sick, you'll be lucky.

Children are naturally noisy and naturally trusting. They will run into the pasture and frighten the horses into running every which way including into the fence (here come the scratches and cuts) or over the fence (here you go again chasing down the road after that darn horse). Of course, after a while, most horses learn to ignore children's odd behavior. But it doesn't happen in one day. It is up to the parent either to find a horse accustomed to children already, or to teach the child to approach the horse quietly at all times. At any rate, he must be taught that all horses are not as nice as yours.

A child should be taught to approach a horse from the front if at all possible. He should be taught always to speak quietly to the horse when approaching from any angle, for the horse may be dozing and not know he is coming. A startled horse jumps first and thinks later. It doesn't take much effort on the part of a horse to throw a man and hurt him badly. Caution around all horses is essential.

Our first horse acquisition was our pony Lucky. We made sure that a gentler pony could not be found. Fundamentally, we looked to see that he did not kick, did not bite, and could stand surprises. It was fortunate that we did. Despite our warnings, the first thing our son Dan did was to approach the pony from the rear and give him a good solid smack on the rump. Not so nice a pony would have flung out and let him have it.

Lucky was our trial and error period. He was so gentle and quiet he even let us tether him to the dog's chain. The children would bring him up to the yard where he was used as third base. The rules of the game were the same as baseball except that when the children reached third base, they had to leapfrog over the pony on their way home. The leapfrogging I put a stop to, but Lucky seemed to like all the activity so he was allowed

Children are naturally trusting.

to remain as third base. Eventually, Lucky would make his way over to the pitcher's mound. Then time was called and third base was moved back to his proper position.

Our wonderful pony would lie down to rest and the children would lie down with him and braid flowers in his mane.

All of this was beautiful and touching to see; but our little Lucky was a rare one, indeed. It took a good year or so of constant reminding to teach our children that he was a pony, not a dog, and must be treated as such. Until the children learned a few manners, we thought it wiser not to get another horse for them.

Teach children never to feed a horse outside of his feeding period except as a reward. Most horses love apples, sugar, and carrots. If the horse or pony knows that the child always carries goodies around, he will start nibbling at the pockets where they are kept. When this happens some people think his trick is cute. The problem is that the horse gets braver and braver with his owner's approval. He may shove or bite or even knock the child over in his hurry to get his tidbit. But he won't stop there. He'll keep shoving and pushing until he gets his treat. In the meantime, the child could be hurt. Don't ever let it start. If you want to give your horse a treat, leave it in his feeder. This will encourage him to enter the barn willingly and will discourage any foolishness in the pasture. Do give horses a treat after each ride if you like. But that is all. Don't be consistent otherwise and don't give treats by hand.

Don't allow your child to walk into a strange pasture unless a person in authority gives permission. I will never forget as a small child being chased up an apple tree by a mare who did not like people. My shortcut turned out to be a long one because the mare never left the bottom of the tree until her owner came to bring her in for her night's feeding. I had several hours to reflect upon my foolishness and to thank my lucky stars there was a tree to climb. If your child is small, do not allow him in your own pasture without an adult, and never allow his friends. Lawsuits could follow.

A good rule of safety is to have a child use the buddy system while out riding. If this isn't possible, know the route the child is taking and approximately how long it takes. Unforeseen accidents can happen anywhere, anytime, even on the safest of horses. I have a scar over my left eye to prove it.

If a child must travel along a road, make sure the horse is familiar with roads. When we first got Pushover, he was more afraid of cars than we were aware. You can imagine my horror when the children returned from their ride laughing because our horse was chasing cars "just like a dog, Mommy." Needless to say, we made a point of exposing Push to all kinds of traffic with an experienced rider on his back. He still bounces when a particularly noisy truck goes by but he is relatively safe now, and more important, the children realize the seriousness of the situation and have learned how to control it.

Impress upon children the importance of regulating the pace of their ride and using good judgment. Make them see the hazards of galloping on a paved road. Make them understand that horses get tired, too, and need a breather. Teach them a set of safety rules. A child's attention span is short. It is only through repeated reminders that he will learn.

Most children like to participate in horse shows. Unless a child has been placed with a professional horseman who is responsible for him and his horse, be aware that the parent will be needed to assist the child in many ways. At the least, he needs his parents' assurance and confidence.

Don't allow a child to be unduly embarrassed. See that he and his horse are dressed correctly for the classes he wishes to enter. Major horse shows are rated A, B, and C. Many small shows are non-rated and just for fun. The A division show usually has the top-rated horses and riders from the area. If a child is a beginning show rider, look for the C-rated or non-rated show to allow him to learn and to gain experience and confidence. Make sure the child knows thoroughly what is expected of both him and his horse and don't let him enter the ring unless you are sure they can do what is required well.

Warn a child that his horse may become nervous and as a result misbehave in this new situation. There are some horses who never do settle down in a show atmosphere.

Prepare yourself for a child's set of nerves. Many children enter the show ring and promptly forget everything they have ever learned. I know lots of adults who do the same thing. Don't despair and don't let him despair. Experience will help.

See that a child honestly realizes that not everyone can win a ribbon. He must accept the judge's decision no matter how disappointed he may be. The child may be inclined to blame everyone but himself. Remind him that there is always a next time, and maybe next time the judge will like him and his horse.

Horse shows are fun but they are also long and tiring. Sometimes there is a long time between the classes in which a child is entered. You and he will probably end up taking turns holding and leading the horse around while you wait. If you know it's to be a long day, try to arrange a place close by where your horse may be stabled in order to give yourselves some free time to enjoy the show and for your horse to rest. Some riders have their own trailers and keep their horses there when they're not using them. Do bring hay and water along to help keep the horse comfortable. Don't be surprised if your child evaporates into thin air, leaving you in sole control of his horse for a very long time. I don't know of a parent that this hasn't happened to until they have learned to avoid it, either by making stabling arrangements or, quite sensibly, by learning to disappear first.

Because horses are becoming increasingly popular, there are more and more organized activities available for children. There are two clubs that are prominent throughout the United States. One is the 4-H Horse Project. The 4-H teaches the child from nine to nineteen how to ride and care for his horse. The other club is the Pony Club. This club originated in England and is principally for English seat riders up to the age of twenty-one. It, too, stresses not only the child's riding ability, but the importance of caring for and feeding a horse correctly. Although it is called the Pony Club, horse-riding children are more in evidence.

Either club will help a child learn about and love his horse. At the same time, the child will find friends who enjoy the same interests, which will in turn encourage him to continue in one of the oldest and finest of sports.

15

A Final Word

I do not want to discourage anyone from riding or owning a horse. I love horses and cannot imagine a life in which they were not an important part. But somehow, some way, people must come to realize that a horse is a living, feeling animal, not just a means to get from point A to point B. I continually see and hear about injustices done to animals.

Just recently I heard about a man who was literally on the way to killing his horse with kindness. He believed that because it was so cold in winter, his horse needed more feed to keep up his strength than he required in the spring or summer. The owner did not take into consideration the fact that the horse was idle during the winter months. Fortunately, the horse had not yet become foundered. However, he did become unruly, high-spirited, and eventually uncontrollable. The owner finally had to sell the horse because he could no longer ride him. The new owner is now suffering with the bad manners the horse learned during his idle period.

I know of another man who did founder his horse. The horse got loose in the barn one night and helped himself to the grain. The next morning the owner found the animal obviously suffering. So he gave the horse *more* grain. It was almost too late when the vet was finally called.

We recently acquired a horse who had been turned out to pasture for a year. The horse, a once coddled racehorse, knew nothing of survival in a pasture and his owner didn't know how or he didn't wish to take the extra time to help protect the horse until he learned to make his own way. As a result, he now looks the picture of Ichabod Crane's horse—all bones and angles. We believe it will take a full year to get him back into condition. What a pity it had to happen.

One young child continually gallops his small pony up and down the street. The boy is much too big for the pony and the constant hard riding has taken its toll. Now his parents want a horse for their child because the pony doesn't go fast enough!

I have seen a man beat his horse on the head with a crop because he wouldn't stand still while the man was trying to mount. Eventually the horse wouldn't come anywhere near him without a fight. It was interesting to note that a quiet youngster could mount the animal any time she wished.

I have seen riders bridle their horses with harsher and harsher bits because they have not learned to control them by any other means than by yanking on their mouths. I know the bit may work for a while, but the rider's own ignorance of riding technique will make the horse misbehave again.

There are some riding stables where the horses are fed only when the manager gets around to it. Water is given sparingly and salt is unheard of.

There is no excuse for these acts of cruelty. I believe—or at least hope —that most people would be kinder to their horses, would care for them and ride them better if they only knew what was expected of them. Hence this simple book, with all its warnings and suggestions.

Heed them, and "Good Riding."

Index